U.S Fish & Wildlife Service

I0434971

A Preliminary Biological Assessment of Long Lake National Wildlife Refuge Complex, North Dakota

Biological Technical Publication

BTP-R6006-2006

U.S Fish & Wildlife Service

A Preliminary Biological Assessment of Long Lake National Wildlife Refuge Complex, North Dakota

Biological Technical Publication

BTP-R6006-2006

Murray K. Laubhan[1]

Robert A. Gleason[1]

Gregory A. Knutsen[2]

Rachel A. Laubhan[3]

N. H. Euliss, Jr.[1]

[1] U.S. Geological Survey, Northern Prairie Wildlife Research Center
8711 37th Street SE, Jamestown, ND

[2] U.S. Fish and Wildlife Service, Region 6, Long Lake National Wildlife Refuge Complex, 12000 353rd Street SE, Moffit, ND

[3] U.S. Fish and Wildlife Service, Region 6, Denver, CO

Cover image credit: Title: Canvasback Hen
Alternative Title: *Aythya valisineria*
Creator: Dewhurst, Donna

Author Contact information:

Murray K. Laubhan, U.S. Geological Survey, Northern Prairie Wildlife Research Center, 8711 37th St. SE, Jamestown, ND 58401. Phone: (701) 253-5534, Fax: (701) 253-5553, e-mail: Murray_Laubhan@usgs.gov.

Robert A. Gleason, U.S. Geological Survey, Northern Prairie Wildlife Research Center, 8711 37th St. SE, Jamestown, ND 58401. Phone: (701) 253-5546, Fax: (701) 253-5553, e-mail: Robert_Gleason@usgs.gov.

Gregory A. Knutsen, U.S. Fish and Wildlife Service, Region 6, Long Lake National Wildlife Refuge Complex, 12000 353rd Street SE, Moffit, ND, USA 58560. Phone: (701) 387-4397, e-mail: Gregg_Knutsen@fws.gov.

Rachel A. Laubhan, U.S. Fish and Wildlife Service, Region 6, Northern Prairie Wildlife Research Center, 8711 37th St. SE, Jamestown, ND 58401. Phone: (701) 253-5543, Fax: (701) 253-5553, e-mail: Rachel_Laubhan@ fws.gov.

N. H. Euliss, Jr., U.S. Geological Survey, Northern Prairie Wildlife Research Center, 8711 37th St. SE, Jamestown, ND 58401. Phone: (701) 253-5564, Fax: (701) 253-5553, e-mail: Ned_Euliss@usgs.gov.

Recommended citation:
Laubhan, M. K, R. A. Gleason, G. A. Knutsen, R. A Laubhan, and Ned H. Euliss, Jr. 2006. *A preliminary biological assessment of Long Lake National Wildlife Refuge Complex, North Dakota.* U.S. Department of Interior, Fish and Wildlife Service, Biological Technical Publication, BTP R6006-2006, Washington, D.C.

For additional copies or information, contact:
Associate Editor: Wayne J. King
Regional Refuge Biologist
USFWS, Region 6
P.O. Box 25486
Denver Federal Center
Denver, Colorado 80225-0486

Table of Contents

List of Figures

List of Tables

Acknowledgments

Prior to writing the report, U.S. Geological Survey personnel (Robert Gleason, Ned Euliss Jr., and Murray Laubhan) were invited to a meeting (5 - 7 April 2004) with Long Lake National Refuge staff (Paul Van Ningen, Gregory Knutsen, Natoma Buskness, and Cheryl Jacobs) and U.S. Fish and Wildlife Service Region 6 personnel (Linda Kelly, Wayne King, Rachel Laubhan, and Adam Misztal). The purpose was to become familiar with certain National Wildlife Refuge lands, discuss management opportunities and constraints, and identify information that potentially could assist the staff in developing a credible biological plan to guide future management. These individuals contributed significant time and insight regarding management of the Long Lake National Wildlife Refuge Complex. Thanks also to the following individuals for providing reviews of an earlier draft: S. L. Jones, D. G. Jorde, W. J. King, D. M. Mushet, J. D. Petty, A. J. Symstad, and K. Torkelson.

Summary

This report represents an initial biological assessment of wetland conditions on Long Lake National Wildlife Refuge (NWR), Slade NWR, and Florence Lake NWR that was conducted as part of the pre-planning phase for development of a Comprehensive Conservation Plan (CCP). According to the 1997 National Wildlife Refuge System Improvement Act (NWRSIA), decisions guiding NWR management should be based on the best available scientific information. Therefore, this report attempts to integrate relevant information from many different scientific disciplines (e.g., geology, hydrology, biology) to assist the U.S. Fish and Wildlife Service (USFWS) in identifying ecological constraints and opportunities imposed by the land base being considered. The intent is to provide information and ideas necessary for evaluating the potential benefits and detriments of management actions during the decision making process that accompanies development of biological goals and objectives.

Information in this report is based on a relatively limited number of published articles, past notes, and observations during a visit to Long Lake, Florence Lake, and Slade NWRs. The authors only attempted to locate sufficient relevant information necessary to formulate more definitive ideas and provide additional context. Thus, the information provided below is incomplete and a more thorough synthesis will be required. Further, interpretation of published information can vary among individuals, and the Long Lake NWR Complex (hereafter Complex) staff is encouraged to review the documents cited in this report. Many years of staff observation and experience managing the Complex are invaluable to ensuring that information used to make decisions is applicable. Consequently, some sections contain information that was not fully explored in the evaluation section; however, the information was retained because it may be useful as the Complex staff and core CCP team examine different management options. Finally, decisions regarding management of the wetland community also require integrating information from terrestrial lands that impact wetlands (i.e. catchment). Although this may seem simple and straightforward, this task often is difficult because it frequently requires an iterative approach to ensure that important issues that may affect management of both wetlands and uplands have not been omitted.

This report does not contain conclusions, nor does it advocate any opinions (favorable or unfavorable) regarding the biological program. Further, concepts such as alternatives, goals, and objectives, are not discussed. The core CCP team will address these topics. Rather, it represents a summary that hopefully will be used to focus future discussion regarding biological data needs and approaches for using this information to make decisions. Ultimately, however, scientific information alone will not lead to a definitive decision regarding future direction. Also, biology is only one of many components that must be considered in the evaluation. Therefore, it is recommended that USFWS personnel responsible for determining the future direction of Complex management be consulted to establish guidelines and agree on the approach that will be used in evaluating the biological program prior to proceeding.

Introduction

The impetus for this report was passage of the 1997 NWRSIA that requires each NWR in the National Wildlife Refuge System (NWRS) to develop a CCP that includes goals and objectives that are based on the best available science. To accomplish this mandate, Region 6 of the USFWS contracted with the Biological Resources Division of the U.S. Geological Survey (USGS) to inspect wetland habitats and synthesize available information pertinent to the management of Long Lake, Slade, and Florence Lake NWRs as part of a pre-planning phase to guide development of a CCP. This report represents the initial synthesis.

The brevity of the site visit did not allow for detailed discussions between USGS and USFWS personnel, but it did provide the opportunity to exchange thoughts regarding the information needed to evaluate the biological program. Thus, the ideas contained within this report are of a general nature and should be viewed as a collaborative effort that involved the Complex staff. Additional work will be required to objectively evaluate the biological program, and this report should be viewed as an initial effort to start this process. In addition, there are alternative ways of approaching an evaluation that would require different levels and types of information. Therefore, the responsibility of the USFWS is to review the report and other relevant materials, discuss available options with appropriate personnel, and determine if the identified information needs and recommendations outlined in this report are acceptable and represent the preferred manner of proceeding.

General descriptive information on NWR establishment, topography, climate, geology, soils, vegetation, and wildlife is intended to provide a brief background of these three NWRs with regard to functions, processes, and values. The scientific names of plants and animals used in the text are provided in Appendix A. This information is important as a baseline for understanding the impact of past land alterations and for developing guidelines for future management. In contrast, the section on wildlife conservation is intended to provide perspective regarding potential NWR contributions to natural resources based on conservation plans that have been developed for application at larger geographic scales that encompass the NWR. The section on evaluation of the wetland community discusses in more detail the processes impacting current wetland conditions. Included in this discussion are terrestrial habitats within the catchment because many biological features of importance in wetlands (e.g., plants, invertebrates) are impacted by processes (e.g., surface runoff, water quality, erosion and deposition of sediment) that originate in the uplands. The intent is to provide thoughts regarding potential information that will assist the USFWS in developing achievable biological objectives during CCP development. The recommendations are largely those of the authors and are based on thoughts that resulted from discussions with USFWS personnel during the site visit. Further, the information needs identified are known to be incomplete from a biological perspective and largely ignore recreational and other considerations. Thus, additional effort will be required by USFWS personnel to identify and integrate issues, concerns, and recommendations through internal discussions and public scoping.

Description

Refuge Establishments and Authorities

All three NWRs considered in this report were established under Executive Order and are managed under authority of the National Wildlife Refuge Administration Act and all other authorities established by legislation pertaining to the NWRS. Long Lake NWR (9025 ha) is managed as a separate unit, whereas, Slade (1214 ha) and Florence Lake (764 ha) NWRs are considered part of the Long Lake Wetland Management District (WMD), a three-county (Burleigh, Kidder, Emmons) area in south-central North Dakota. In addition to Slade and Florence Lake NWRs, the 69,580-ha WMD also includes 80 waterfowl production areas ([WPA], 8711 ha), 1013 wetland easements (40,646 ha), six easement NWRs (2342 ha), 43 grassland easements (6556 ha), and one wildlife development area (WDA; 321 ha). The WDA was purchased and developed by the Bureau of Reclamation and transferred to the USFWS in 1991 for management as a mitigation obligation of the Garrison Diversion Project (URL http://longlake.fws.gov/Wmd.htm). The NWR purposes are based on land acquisition documents and authorities only (URL http://refugedata.fws.gov/databases/purpose) and do not include purposes that may be identified in other documents, including deed restrictions, management agreements with primary land managers, and congressional established wilderness designations which were not part of the acquisition documents and authorities.

Long Lake NWR. Established "... as a refuge and breeding ground for migratory birds and other wildlife ..." (Executive Order 8119, dated 10 May 1939), "... for use as an inviolate sanctuary, or for any other management purpose, for migratory birds" (16 U.S.C. § 715d [Migratory Bird Conservation Act]), and "... shall be administered by him [Secretary of the Interior] directly or in accordance with cooperative agreements ... and in accordance with such rules and regulations for the conservation, maintenance, and management of wildlife, resources thereof, and its habitat thereon, ..." (16 U.S.C. § 664 [Fish and Wildlife Coordination Act]).

Slade NWR. Established "... for use as an inviolate sanctuary, or for any other management purpose, for migratory birds" (16 U.S.C. § 715d [Migratory Bird Conservation Act]).

Florence Lake NWR. Established "... as a refuge and breeding ground for migratory birds and other wildlife ..." (Executive Order 8119, dated 10 May 1939), "... for use as an inviolate sanctuary, or for any other management purpose, for migratory birds." (16 U.S.C. § 715d [Migratory Bird Conservation Act]), and "... shall be administered by him [Secretary of the Interior] directly or in accordance with cooperative agreements ... and in accordance with such rules and regulations for the conservation, maintenance, and management of wildlife, resources thereof, and its habitat thereon, ..." (16 U.S.C. § 664 [Fish and Wildlife Coordination Act]).

Location and Formation

All three NWRs are located in south-central North Dakota: Long Lake NWR in Burleigh and Kidder Counties, Slade NWR in Kidder County, and Florence Lake NWR in Burleigh County (Figure 1). This area is part of the Interior Plains major physiographic division, the Great Plains province, and the Glaciated Missouri Plateau section (Fenneman 1931).

Preglacial drainage of the area included the ancestral river systems of the Knife, Cannonball, Heart, and Grand Rivers that trended northeast and flowed into Hudson Bay (Kume and Hansen 1965). The ancient Cannonball River may have been a tributary to the ancestral Red River (Lemke and Colton 1958). At this time, the Missouri River flowed northeast from the northwest corner of North Dakota to Hudson Bay (Flint 1955).

During the Wisconsin Stage of the Pleistocene, ice advanced four and at least three times in Burleigh and Kidder counties, respectively (Rau et al. 1962, Kume and Hansen 1965). The Napoleon ice sheet (Burleigh County only) advanced first, followed by the Long Lake, Burnstad, and Streeter advances in both counties. Each ice advance was halted by buttes and mesas that comprise the eastern border of the Missouri Couteau in central North Dakota and was followed by a period of stagnation and melting (Rau et al. 1962). For example, the Napoleon advance was followed by a period of glacial retreat and erosion that may have lasted more than 25,000 years (Clayton 1962). This activity resulted in the deposition of dead-ice moraine (i.e., landforms composed of hummocky accumulations that are primarily till deposited by glacial ice) behind the end moraines and generated large amounts of outwash (e.g., glaciolacustrine and glaciofluvial sediments) in front of the terminal end point of each advance (Rau et al. 1962). In addition, the ancestral Missouri River was blocked and diverted to the southeast.

The Long Lake advance occurred about 12,000 to 13,000 years ago and deposited end and ground moraine in the eastern and western portions of Burleigh and Kidder counties, respectively. At this time, the valley currently occupied by Long Lake NWR constituted part of the Cannonball River. The preglacial valley was > 1.6 km wide and ranged from 30 to 91 m in depth (Rau et al. 1962). The initial lobes of the Long Lake advance followed bedrock lows and a lobe of ice pushed along the valley of the Cannonball River south of Steele and deposited a great loop of end moraine in the vicinity of Long Lake (Rau et al. 1962). As this glacier retreated, ground moraine was deposited and meltwater flowed through preexisting channels (stream flow was to the south rather than the preglacial direction of northeast) to newly formed glacial lakes McKenzie and Steele (Rau et al. 1962, Kume and Hansen 1965). As further melting occurred, dead-ice moraine was deposited on bedrock highs adjacent to main valleys and the valleys were filled with outwash and ponded sediment because meltwater was confined behind the end moraines that dammed the ancestral rivers (Rau et al. 1962, Kume and Hansen 1965, Bluemle 2000).

About 12,000 years ago, the Burnstad glacier advanced and overrode the Long Lake end moraine in the northern part of Burleigh County and southeastern Kidder County. The margin of the Burnstad glacier stagnated and formed dead-ice moraine. Meltwater transporting outwash from this glacier flowed through Apple Creek, Random Creek, and the Cannonball River channels into Glacial Lake McKenzie and formed an outwash plain in the northern portion of the lake. Cutting and filling on the floodplain of the Missouri River perhaps formed the higher terraces at this time. Finally, the Streeter ice sheet advanced into northern Burleigh and eastern Kidder counties and deposited a number of end moraine loops along its leading edge. As this glacier retreated, a large sheet of outwash was deposited on the older drift from Robinson to Lake George and filled major bedrock valleys with stratified drift (Rau et al. 1962). This outwash collapsed as ice from the Burnstad glacier melted and collapsed. As melting of the Burnstad ice continued, which may have occurred for more than 2,000 years (Clayton 1962), the resulting deposits of dead-ice moraine slowly assumed their present topography. In addition, the amount of meltwater was sufficient to eventually breach the Long Lake end moraine and thereby allow transport of sediment-laden waters to the Missouri River and Glacial Lake McKenzie (Kume and Hansen 1965).

During the Recent Age (5000 years ago to present), the area has been modified by stream erosion and slope wash to establish the present drainage pattern that consists of the Missouri River and its tributaries. The present channel of the Missouri River comprises segments representing preexisting river channels and segments of superposed drainage divide channels. The diverted Missouri River channel captures many east flowing rivers on the Missouri Plateau section, but the tributary pattern is asymmetrical with well developed western tributaries (e.g., Knife, Heart, and Cannonball rivers) and underdeveloped eastern tributaries (Snake, Painted Woods, Burnt, Apple, and Badger creeks). In southern Burleigh and Kidder counties, streams drain into the Long Lake trough, which also contains Lake Etta and Lake Isabel, whereas Lake George and Alkali Lake receive discharge from the surface streams in the southeast corner of Kidder County. However, the majority of intermittent streams that originate in the end, dead-ice, and recessional moraines flow into small lakes and sloughs or disappear by infiltration into outwash.

Landform and Topography
The Glaciated Plains section is comprised of several subdivisions; however, the number and boundaries of subdivisions vary depending on the source consulted (Fennemen 1931, Clayton 1962, Lemke and Colton 1958, Kume and Hansen 1965). This report adheres to the boundaries proposed by Kume and Hansen (1965), which places Long Lake and Slade NWRs in the Long Lake Basin subdistrict of the Coteau Slope district and Florence Lake NWR in the Missouri Coteau district. The Coteau Slope district is characterized by streams that are predominantly intermittent or ephemeral and drainage that is internal and partially integrated. The area is subject to active erosion by integrated streams that discharge to the Missouri River (Kume and Hansen 1965). Drift in this area is largely from the early Wisconsin and thickness ranges from moderate to nonexistent (Clayton 1962). More specifically, the Long Lake Basin subdistrict largely is composed of outwash and lake plain. Ground moraine flanks outwash on the north and south sides of Long Lake. The till (i.e., generally fine-grained, unstratified, and unsorted material of various types that ranges in size from clays to boulders) of this moraine is sandy and pebbly, and exhibits a low undulating surface that extends from the outwash plain adjacent to Long Lake toward the end moraine at higher elevations (Kume and Hansen 1965).

Long Lake NWR, as well as Lake Etta and Lake Isabel, is situated in the partially buried valley of the ancestral Cannonball River. The depth to bedrock in the main valley of the ancestral Cannonball River between Long Lake and Lake Etta was 91 m and the difference in elevation between the depth to bedrock on the old upland surface at Steele, North Dakota, and the floor of the Cannonball south of this location was > 145 m prior to glaciation. Thus, the preglacial surface exhibited considerable relief and must have resembled the bluffs that flank the Missouri River trench (Rau et al. 1962). In contrast, elevations in the basin following glaciation range from about 549 m at the edge to about 518 m in the center (Kume and Hansen 1965). Thickness of the valley fills range from 38 to 51 m in Burleigh County to 91 m in Kidder County. Surface deposits are mostly sand, but clay deposits also are common.

The Missouri Coteau district, which encompasses Florence Lake NWR, is characterized by non-integrated drainage and numerous undrained depressions. The few streams that exist in the district are of short length, tend to exhibit ephemeral flows, and typically drain into nearby lakes and kettles. Drift largely is from the Late Wisconsin and thickness of glacial till ranges from a feather edge to 50 m (average = 18 m). The area is dominated by extensive dead-ice moraine and associated stagnant ice-disintegration features, including numerous kettles, disintegration ridges and trenches, and kames (Kume and Hansen 1965). The dead-ice moraine occurs at elevations ranging from 661 to 640 m) and maximum relief is about 30 m. Another glacial landform in the district is collapsed outwash topography (i.e., landforms composed of hummocky accumulations of stratified, primarily glaciofluvial drift sediment), which contains abundant kettles and other ice-contact features. Embedded within the collapsed outwash topography are numerous saline and fresh lakes, including Florence Lake (Kume and Hansen 1965). Topography has been influenced by glacial activity that reduced the local bedrock relief by abrading and reducing the elevation of higher bedrock areas and differentially filling valleys with glacial drift. The maximum relief in Kidder County is 152 m, but local relief varies from 3 to 15 m. Elevations on the collapsed outwash range between 561 and 579 m.

Soils
Information in this section represents a general summary intended to outline general soil characteristics.

The bedrock in Burleigh County consists of 2438 m of Paleozoic, Mesozoic, and Cenozoic sedimentary rocks. The Surface bedrock includes the Late Cretaceous Pierre (marine shale), Fox Hills (marine sandstone), and Hell Creek (sandstone, mudstone, siltstone, lignite, carbonaceous shale) Formations, and the Tertiary Paleocene Fort Union Group consisting of the Ludlow (continental sandstone, lignite, and shale), Cannonball (marine sandstone, siltstone, shale, and limestone), and Tongue River (continental sandstone, claystone, siltstone, shale, limestone, and lignite) Formations (Kume and Hansen 1965). Beneath the glacial drift in Kidder County, the uppermost bedrock includes the Pierre and Fox Hills Formations of the Late Cretaceous and the Cannonball and Tongue River Formations of the Fort Union Group (Rau et al. 1962).

The glacial till that overlies most of the surface bedrock in Kidder and Burleigh counties is similar with respect to physical characteristics. There are no significant differences in size, and differences in color and pebble composition are subtle (Rau et al. 1962, Kume and Hansen 1965). Grain size analyses of 47 samples from Kidder County indicate the sand, silt, and clay percentages of till range from about 1.0 – 58.5, 22.0 – 45.0, and 18.9 – 77.0, respectively. However, if two samples are excluded, ranges of grain size are 24.0 – 58.5%

sand, 13.3 – 45.0% silt, and 18.9 – 46.8% clay, respectively (Rau et al. 1962), which is similar to the grain analyses of 34 till samples in Burleigh County (18.0 – 50.4% sand, 23.8 – 41.6% silt, and 23.5 – 49.9% clay) (Kume and Hansen 1965). Most of the till in Kidder County has reddish-yellow spots caused by oxidation of iron oxide originating from Pierre Shale, and a white mottling caused by concentration of calcium carbonate (Rau et al. 1962). In Burleigh County, oxidized till occurs to depths of 6 to 9 m and exhibits a mottled appearance due to calcium carbonate concentrations. In addition, free pebbles are frequently encrusted with caliche and particles of shale and lignite are common (Kume and Hansen 1965). In contrast, glaciofluvial sediments in both Kidder and Burleigh counties are comprised primarily of stratified sands and gravel that range in size from fine sand to pebbles, whereas glaciolacustrine sediments primarily consist of silts and clays.

The principal parent materials of soils on all three NWRs are glacial till, glacial outwash, and sediments of glaciolacustrine and glaciofluvial origin. The physical and mineralogical properties of this parent material, in combination with long-term climatic regimes, have greatly influenced the physical and chemical properties of soils. Taxonomically, soils within the boundaries of the three NWRs belong to more than 20 series (Table 1) and nine subgroups (typic and pachic Argiborolls; typic, entic, pachic, and udic Haploborolls; typic Ustipsamments; typic Natraquolls; and typic Psammaquents) (Stout et al. 1974, Seelig and Gulsvig 1988). These soil series form 10 associations (i.e., areas with a proportional pattern of soils that normally consist of one or more major soils and at least one minor soil) that comprise the terrestrial land base of these three NWRs. Of these, the dominant associations on all three NWRs are loams and sands derived from glacial outwash and glacial till that typically are deep, medium to moderately coarse in texture, range in available water capacity from very low to high, and are susceptible to erosion by either wind or water (Stout et al. 1974, Seelig and Gulsvig 1988). Soils underlying uplands on Long Lake NWR are sands and clays, whereas most soils underlying uplands on Slade NWR and Florence Lake NWR are a sand-silt mix and sandy loam underlain by gravel, respectively (URL http://longlake.fws.gov/). With the exception of the Lehr-Wabek-Manning (nearly level to steep) and Harriet-Minnewaukon-Stirum (level) associations, all other soil associations occur in areas topographically characterized as nearly level to rolling or gently rolling. Within each association, individual soil series typically can be arranged based on slope position.

Wetland features do not occupy a large proportion of the area considered at the scale of an association; thus, soils underlying wetlands (e.g., depression, basins, swales, shallow drainages) are not adequately represented at the level of the soil association. In addition, soil associations do not adequately address the soils derived from glaciolacustrine and glaciofluvial sediments that underlay lakes within the boundaries of the three NWRs (Stout et al. 1974). Soils in these series often have unique characteristics, including highly calcareous soils (e.g., Arveson and Colvin series), dense alkali subsoil (e.g., Noonan series) and the presence of claypans (e.g., Belfield, Daglum, and Rhoades series). As a result, soils underlying wetlands often exhibit very different properties compared to the major soils composing an association; thus, characteristics of individual soil series must be evaluated (Table 2). In general, soils in these series exhibit very slow to only moderate permeability, moderate to high available water capacity, moderate to high organic matter content, and medium to high fertility.

Climate

The climate of North Dakota is continental (Rosenberg 1987, Harrington and Harman 1995), and is characterized by relatively short, moderately hot summers and relatively long, cold winters (Kantrud et al. 1989). Other general climatic features of the state include large annual and daily temperature fluctuations, light to moderate annual precipitation that varies in time of occurrence, low relative humidity, and nearly continuous air movement (Jensen undated). This large variation is due primarily to geographic location. The Rocky Mountains act as a barrier to the prevailing westerly flow of atmospheric air and modify Pacific Ocean air masses from cool and moist to mild and dry. In contrast, cold, dry air masses originating in northern Polar Regions and warm, moist air masses from the Gulf of Mexico easily overflow North Dakota because mountain barriers are lacking. Thus, the climate of the state is influenced by cold, dry air masses from Polar Regions, warm, moist air masses from tropical regions, and mild, dry air masses from the northern Pacific (Lemke 1960). These air masses flow through North Dakota during every season and typically progress rapidly, which causes frequent and rapid weather changes.

Climate information in this report was obtained from weather station 326015 operated by the High Plains Regional Climate Center (URL http://www. hprcc.unl.edu/) located at Moffit, North Dakota. Depending on the variables of interest, data for this station are available from 1948 to 2004. The average annual temperature is 6.1° C, but the average annual minimum and maximum temperatures range from -1.4° to 13.0° C. Based on long-term monthly averages, January is the coldest month (mean = -12.4° C), followed by February (-8.7° C) and December (-8.7° C), whereas the warmest months are June (18.6° C), July (21.4° C), and August (21.0° C). Further, the annual average number of days with maximum and minimum temperatures of > 32.2° C and < 0° C, respectively, is 25 and 73. However, differences between monthly average minimum and maximum temperatures are as much as 11 to 17° C. The growing season, defined as the long-term average number of consecutive days that the minimum temperature does not fall below 0° C, ranges from 99 to 147, which correlates well with

an average frost-free period of 120 days reported for central North Dakota (Winter et al. 1984). The average dates of last spring and first fall frosts in Kidder County are 24 May and 13 September, respectively, and average frost penetration is about 1.2 m (Lemke 1960, Rau et al. 1962).

Average annual total precipitation is 40.6 cm, of which 73% (30.2 cm) occurs primarily as rain from May through September. In contrast, the average annual lake evaporation ranges from 83.8 to 102.0 cm (Shjeflo 1968, Kantrud et al. 1989). Thus, the region exhibits a negative precipitation:evaporation ratio and lands in Burleigh and Kidder counties are considered semiarid (Rau et al. 1962, Kume and Hansen 1965). The annual average number of days with precipitation events that are > 0.03 cm and > 0.3 cm are 71 and 35, respectively. In summer, most rainfall is associated with thunderstorms (average = 25 to 35 days per year) (Shjeflo 1968). In most years, at least some part of the state experiences a severe storm that produces 5.1 to 7.6 cm of rain in 24 hrs, and occasionally 12.7 to 15.2 cm or more can occur in one day (Jensen undated). At Moffit, the largest single day precipitation event was 11.9 cm. In contrast, average monthly precipitation during winter is only 2.4 cm and occurs mostly as snow. Despite the northerly location, average annual statewide snowfall is only 63.5 - 114.3 cm, which is less than other northern states.

Ground Water and Surface Water

Essentially all water in this region is derived from precipitation; however, some portion of this water enters the ground through direct or indirect percolation or is transported along the ground surface to topographically lower areas. For example, many river and stream valleys function to collect excess surface water that cannot be absorbed into soils at local scales. In general, ground water is abundant in both Burleigh and Kidder counties (Rau et al. 1962, Kume and Hansen 1965). However, the amount of ground-water recharge that occurs varies locally and depends on numerous factors, including topography, climatic variables (e.g., precipitation and temperature patterns), and soil characteristics (e.g., available water capacity). In general, ground-water recharge tends to be greatest during periods of major precipitation that result in large amounts of surface runoff (Randich and Hatchett 1966). Further, areas dominated by alluvium (e.g., many wetland features) and glaciofluvial silts, sands, and gravels (e.g., valleys or channels that historically transported glacial melt-water runoff) are permeable and capable of collecting, transmitting, and storing water (alluvium = 189 liters per minute [lpm], glaciofluvial sediment yields = 568 – 3785 lpm). In contrast, lacustrine deposits comprised of sandy silts and clays can collect and store large quantities of water, but are generally of limited permeability and yield only small quantities of water (Randich and Hatchett 1966). Therefore, the largest aquifers are located in the sands and gravels in the Missouri River terraces and buried drainage channels, but smaller aquifers also exist in the sandstones and sands of the Fox Hills, Hell Creek, Cannonball, and Tongue River Formations (Randich and Hatchett 1966).

The chemical quality of ground water varies among aquifers and locally depending on numerous factors, including the materials water contacts in the atmosphere and soil, extent of bacterial activity, soil properties (e.g., base exchange), and the physical interaction of surface water with ground-water flow systems (Randich and Hatchett 1966, Lissey 1971, Winter 1977, Swanson et al. 1988). Although limited, available water quality data obtained from wells (domestic and stock) within or near each of the NWRs suggest differences occur within and among sites with different geologic material (Table 3). For example, the specific conductance of ground water on Long Lake NWR ranged from 734 mmhos per cm in glacial drift to 2496 mmhos per cm in Foxhills sandstone, whereas concentrations of sulfate ranged from 2.7 ppm in Foxhills sandstone to 131.0 ppm in glacial outwash. Differences also exist within the same material on Long Lake NWR. For example, concentrations of sodium and bicarbonate in ground water collected from glacial drift material ranged from 33 to 246 ppm and 329 to 641 ppm, respectively (Randich et al. 1962, Randich and Hatchett 1966, Table 3).

In general, the chemistry of precipitation is relatively free of contaminants. However, as excess rainwater (i.e., above soil saturation) is transported across the soil surface (i.e., runoff) it can accumulate various materials (e.g., agrichemicals) prior to discharging into a wetland basin. The concentration of these constituents is further modified by climate. For example, all three NWRs are located in a climatic zone characterized by a negative precipitation:evaporation ratio that concentrates chemical constituents seasonally and intra-annually due to evapotranspiration. Thus, the surface water chemistry of wetlands tends to be dynamic because of complex interactions among numerous factors, including the position of the wetland in relation to ground-water flow systems, chemical composition of ground water, surrounding land uses, and climate (LaBaugh et al. 1987, Swanson et al. 1988, Winter 2003). Given the variability within and among wetland basins, it is not possible to provide a general characterization of surface water quality for these three NWRs. However, water quality of all three units of Long Lake NWR has been recorded previously. In May of 1969, several water quality parameters were collected at the following locations: (1) on the east and west sides of a road crossing Long Lake, (2) Upper Harker and Harker lakes on Slade NWR, and (3) Lake Isabel that adjoins Slade NWR on the west (Swanson et al. 1988). The pH of water at both Long Lake locations was about 9.0, total alkalinity (mg per L) was 480 (west) and 860 (east), specific conductance (μS per cm) was 1560 (west) and 4150 (east), and sulfate concentration (mg per L) was 900 (west) and 1185 (east). In contrast, the pH of water in lakes on Slade NWR ranged from 8.7 (Upper Harker) to 9.3 (Harker), total alkalinity

(mg per L) ranged from 950 (Upper Harker) to 1540 (Harker), specific conductance (μS per cm) ranged from 2300 (Isabel) to 4700 (Harker), and sulfate concentrations (mg per L) ranged from 350 (Isabel) to 1050 (Harker). Although quantitative reports of water quality were not located for Florence Lake NWR, the values obtained illustrate the differences that can occur among lakes within similar physiographic areas (e.g., subdistricts, districts). In addition, differences can occur within different portions of the same basin. For example, in April 2004 the specific conductance (μS per cm) of water in Long Lake NWR Unit 1, Unit 2, and Unit 3 was 1910, 2600, and 4200, respectively (RAG).

In March of 1989, another water quality study was conducted on Long Lake NWR (Olson and Welsh 1991). Complete data from this report were not located, but concentrations of certain elements were provided. In general, the alkalinity and nutrient concentrations of Long Lake surface water were high, which is typical of prairie lakes in this region; however, elevated mercury and boron concentrations and high sodium concentrations also were documented (Swanson et al. 1988). Given the alkalinity of the lake, however, the observed mercury concentrations in surface waters would not be readily activated biologically.

Vegetation
Historically, the landscape of south-central North Dakota was characterized by numerous wetlands embedded in a background matrix of northern mixed-grass prairie (Fennemen 1931). Distribution and density of wetlands was correlated with various glacial landforms in the region. The greatest area of semipermanent palustrine wetlands occurred in areas of dead-ice and terminal moraine (e.g., Missouri Coteau), whereas the greatest area of temporary and seasonal wetlands occurred in the ground moraine and lake plain (Kantrud et al. 1989). In contrast, rivers and lakes occurred predominantly in topographically low areas that transported meltwater from retreating glaciers.

The composition of vegetation in wetlands changes dynamically in response to numerous factors, including short- and long-term hydroperiods and water chemistry (Kantrud et al. 1989, Euliss et al. 2004). Most palustrine basins exhibit concentric zones of vegetation that are dominated by different plant species (Kantrud et al. 1989). The most commonly used terms to refer to these zones are, in decreasing order of water permanency, deep marsh, shallow marsh, and wet meadow (Kantrud et al. 1989). The water regime in a deep marsh zone usually is semipermanent. Dominant plants include cattail, bulrush, submersed or floating plants, and submersed vascular plants, but this zone also may be devoid of vegetation if bottom sediments are unconsolidated. Shallow marsh zones usually are dominated by emergent grasses, sedges, and some forbs, but submersed or floating vascular plants also may occur. Wet meadow zones also are typically dominated by grasses, rushes, and sedges, but submersed or floating plants are absent. The primary difference between these zones is hydroperiod. Surface flooding of the shallow marsh zone usually is seasonal and ranges from spring to mid- or late summer. In contrast, inundation of the wet meadow zone typically is only temporary (e.g., one to several weeks in spring or briefly after heavy summer rains).

The gradient from fresh to hypersaline water is a continuum, and any divisions are arbitrary (Euliss et al. 2004). In addition, salinity levels can fluctuate widely within and among seasons (Stewart and Kantrud 1972). In general, however, surface water in temporary and seasonal wetland basins is usually fresh (< 500 micromhos per cm) or slightly brackish (500 - 2000 micromhos per cm), whereas semipermanently flooded basins are often brackish (5000 – 15,000 micromhos per cm), but can range from fresh to subsaline (1500 0- 45,000 micromhos per cm) (Stewart and Kantrud 1971). Although the general effect of increased salinity in any zone of wetland vegetation is a decrease in species diversity, it is difficult to establish meaningful salinity tolerances for individual species in their natural habitats because of the complex interaction of abiotic factors. However, general estimates of salinity tolerance are available for numerous emergent and aquatic plant species (Kantrud et al. 1989).

Uplands historically were comprised of warm-season grasses characteristic of both the short-grass prairie and the cool- and warm-season grasses characteristic of the tall-grass prairie (Samson et al. 1998); thus, the area represented a zone of ecotonal mixing that included a diversity of short, intermediate, and tall grass species (Bragg and Steuter 1996). Vegetation composition at regional and local scales was determined by numerous interrelated factors, including elevation, topography, climate, soil characteristics, herbivory, and fire (Hanson and Whitman 1938, Coupland 1950, URL http://www.worldwildlife.org/wildworld/profiles/terrestrial/na/na0810_full.html). The mixed-grass prairie in North Dakota has been classified into nine major vegetation types based primarily on plant species composition and topography (Hanson and Whitman 1938). Species typical of all these types include western wheatgrass, blue grama, prairie junegrass, needle-and-thread, Sandberg's bluegrass, little bluestem, needleleaf sedge, and threadleaf sedge (Whitman 1941, Kantrud and Kologiski 1982).

However, even within a vegetation type, local variation exists. For example, in xeric areas the blue grama, needle-and-thread, and threadleaf sedge association also included western wheatgrass, prairie junegrass, and needleleaf sedge as less important dominant grasses and about 12 dominant forbs (e.g., lotus milkvetch, narrowleaf goosefoot, scarlet beeblossom, flatspine stickseed, stiffstem flax, spiny phlox, woolly plantain) (Hanson and Whitman 1938, Coupland 1992). In contrast, more mesic areas in the same association supported more slender wheatgrass, fendler threeawn, sideoats

grama, little bluestem, porcupine grass, green needlegrass, and sun sedge, whereas dominant forbs included tarragon, prairie sagewort, white sagebrush, blacksamson echinacea, and white milkwort (Sarvis 1920). Other associations include those on sandy loams and fine sandy loams that typically occurred on topographically high areas, as well as those that tended to occur in depressional areas dominated by silt loams and silty clay loams characterized by increased soil moisture and high concentrations of carbonates and soluble salts. The former were dominated by grasses in the *Bouteloua* (grama) and *Stipa* (needle-and-thread, green needle, porcupine) genera, and sedges in the Carex genus, whereas the latter were characterized by species such as inland saltgrass, Nuttall's alkaligrass, and foxtail barley (Hanson and Whitman 1938).

Human alteration (e.g., conversion to agricultural production) of the landscape has resulted in the loss of > 50% of wetlands (Dahl 1990) and 68% of mixed-grass prairie in North Dakota (Samson et al. 1998). The current total wetland area is 38,342 and 52,831 ha, respectively, in Burleigh and Kidder counties (Reynolds et al. 1997, Table 4). Semipermanent wetlands (11,952 ha) and lakes (24,313 ha) constitute the greatest wetland area in Burleigh and Kidder counties, respectively; however, seasonal wetlands occur in the highest density in both counties (Burleigh County = 6.16 per km2, Kidder County = 6.66 per km^2) (Reynolds et al. 1997). Further, approximately 68% of the land in the counties (Burleigh, Kidder, and Emmons) that comprise all three NWRs and the WMD remains in native grassland (URL http://mountain-prairie.fws.gov/reference/briefing_book_nd_2000.pdf). However, in addition to habitat loss and fragmentation, the ecological processes determining the structure and function of remaining native communities also have been severely impacted. For example, the World Wildlife Organization considers the mixed-grass prairie among the most disturbed of all grassland ecoregions; only a few remnant patches remain and none are considered intact (URL http://www.worldwildlife.org/wildworld/profiles/terrestrial/na/na0810_full.html). Major perturbations include altered hydrology (e.g., ground water withdrawal, construction of dams), the use of pesticides (e.g., in 1991 more than 100,000 metric tons applied in the mid-continent; Samson et al. 1998), cessation or alteration of historic burning regimes, modified animal communities, and introduction of exotic plants.

The above impacts are evident on portions of each NWR considered in this report. Most lakes and wetlands occurring on Long Lake NWR are located in and along the distal side of morainal areas that exhibit nonintegrated drainage. Water in these areas is collected locally and dissipates primarily by evapotranspiration and percolation into the water table. However, following purchase by the USFWS in the 1930s, the Civilian Conservation Corps (CCC) constructed three dikes to control water levels in Long Lake, built several small dams across ravines that discharged water to Long Lake for the purpose of ponding water in additional areas, and constructed 19 duck nesting islands in Units 1 and 2 of Long Lake (URL http://longlake.fws.gov/History.IITM). Many upland areas purchased as part of Long Lake NWR previously had been cultivated under private ownership. After acquisition by the USFWS, some of these lands continued to be cultivated, some were planted with tame grass mixes, and most continued to be invaded by noxious exotic plants (e.g., Canada thistle, absinth wormwood).

The current composition of wetlands on Long Lake NWR (total = 7096 ha), based on National Wetland Inventory (NWI) data provided by Complex staff, includes lakes (6558 ha), semipermanent wetlands (187 ha), seasonal wetlands (25 ha), temporary wetlands (116 ha), and riverine habitat (6 ha, Table 5). In addition, Complex staff completed a habitat inventory in 2003 that recorded 34 wetlands (11.2 ha) not classified by NWI. Long Lake, a 6071-ha alkaline basin, is the predominant wetland on Long Lake NWR. The remaining wetland area consists of Long Lake Creek (riverine), natural wetlands, dugouts, and man-made impoundments. Water-level management is the primary strategy used to manipulate wetland conditions on Long Lake and adjacent marshes, but control often is limited. For example, in some years water can be transported to Unit 2 Marsh via gravity flow or pumping, but dewatering can only occur by evapotranspiration.

The vegetation composition of wetlands on Long Lake NWR is dynamic as evidenced by past reports and observations of Complex staff. For example, the presence of single-celled green algae, blue-green algae, and phytoplankton (diatoms and cyanobacteria) have been reported previously (Metcalf 1931, Olson and Welsh 1991) and a plant survey conducted in 1917 indicated that abundant emergent plant species in Long Lake included cosmopolitan bulrush, tule bulrush, and three-square bulrush. This survey also reported common spikerush as common, seaside arrowgrass, prairie cordgrass, and common bladderwort as fairly common, and softstem bulrush as rare (Metcalf 1931). In addition, aerial photographs of Long Lake indicate dense stands of emergent growth, including many species mentioned in the 1917 survey, have been present in the units during past years (GAK). During the site visit, algae were evident in the Long Lake units but emergent and submergent vegetation along the perimeter was minimal at the few locations examined. Emergent vegetation in Unit 2 Marsh included bulrush, cattail, common reed, prairie cordgrass, saltgrass, seepweed, kochia, dock, and cocklebur. However, a sufficient number of sites were not visited to adequately characterize the current composition or extent of wetland vegetation and, unfortunately, the Complex staff does not have an established monitoring program that would allow an objective examination of vegetation dynamics in wetlands.

Uplands (total = 1924 ha) on Long Lake NWR are dominated (> 50% cover) by grasses (1531 ha), noxious weeds (56 ha), shrubs (161 ha), trees (19 ha), and crops (142 ha, Table 5). Of the grassland area, about 1416 ha consist of areas dominated by non-native grasses, whereas introduced cool-season grasses and legumes (i.e., dense nesting cover [DNC]) occupies 72 ha). In contrast, the area dominated by natives is only 11 ha and is highly fragmented ($n = 42$ patches) (Table 5). Areas dominated by noxious or invasive weeds other than non-native grasses occur primarily as scattered, small patches. Principal non-grass noxious or invasive weed species are Canada thistle (30 ha) and absinth wormwood (26 ha), with lesser amounts of Russian olive and leafy spurge. Much of the historic cropland on Long Lake NWR has been seeded to native grass mixtures, tame grass, or DNC; however, about 142 ha are still cultivated (small grains = 133 ha, row crops = 9 ha) as part of a seedbed preparation strategy for eventual reseeding to native grasses. For example, approximately 73 ha of farm fields were seeded to native grasses in 2002. Other techniques used to manipulate the species composition and structure of existing herbaceous upland vegetation (native and non-native) includes a combination of haying, grazing, prescribed burning, and, in areas dominated by noxious or invasive plant species, chemical and biocontrol agents.

In addition to the general vegetation characteristics mentioned above, more detailed information on upland plant species composition is available for six priority management units on Long Lake NWR. Permanent belt transects (25-m length) were established in these units using a stratified-random approach and methods (Grant et al. 2004). Strata consisted of three site types (i.e., xeric, northeast slopes, southwest slopes) and, within each unit-strata combination, one transect was established per 4 ha. One of these management units (G-6) was seeded to a mix of cool and warm season native grasses in June 2002; however, only 79% of this 74 ha unit was actually seeded. Based on 900 data points ($n = 18$ belt transects) collected in 2004, the frequency that native and exotic vegetation occurred along transects was 36.2% and 63.8%, respectively. These data also indicate that 6.4% and 59.7% of G-6 currently is moderately and heavily invaded by exotic plants, respectively (Table 6). The other five units are comprised of virgin sod with a similar land use history; thus, data for these units were combined. In 2004, the frequency of native and exotic vegetation occurrence along 74 belt transects ($n = 3700$ points) in these five units was 19.8% and 80.2%, respectively. Further, these data indicate that 22.98% and 61.94% of these units are moderately and heavily invaded by exotic plants, respectively (Table 6).

Prior to USFWS ownership, the land that now comprises Slade NWR was purchased by Mr. Slade in the mid-1920s for a private shooting club. During the drought period of the 1930s, the land was tilled to provide wildlife food, a large well (60,567 L per hr) was dug between Harker and Upper Harker lakes, and a system of pipes and flumes was used to transport water to the lakes. In addition, large quantities of grain were purchased and shipped to the area to provide supplemental food for waterfowl. Currently, wetlands on Slade NWR are comprised of five semipermanent wetlands, 15 temporary or seasonal wetlands, and several manmade wetlands (e.g., dugouts). Total wetland area is about 395 ha, with lakes and marshes predominating. Trees occupy the margin of some wetlands and dead widgeon grass was evident along the shoreline of at least one lake. Other emergent vegetation recorded in seasonal wetlands during the site visit included smartweed, sedges, reed canary grass, and common reed. Additionally, 26 aquatic and semiaquatic plant species were identified during a 1968 survey, including four species of bulrush, six species of rush, narrow-leaved cattail, sprangletop, muskgrass, American milfoil, common bladderwort, and sago pondweed (GAK). There is evidence that the temporary and seasonal wetlands had been farmed prior to NWR establishment.

The balance of land (820 ha) comprising Slade NWR is terrestrial and includes native grassland (81 ha), tame grass (522 ha), shelterbelts (16 ha), and agricultural units (197 ha) (URL http://longlake. fws.gov/Slade.HTM). The dominant tame grasses are smooth brome and Kentucky bluegrass, and the dominant noxious weed is leafy spurge. The majority of farming on the NWR is organic. Terrestrial lands periodically are hayed and grazed, and areas dominated by leafy spurge are treated with a combination of chemicals, biocontrol (e.g., beetles), and haying.

Florence Lake NWR includes 594 ha of fee title and 170 ha of easement land (URL http://longlake.fws. gov/FlorenceLake.HTM). Collectively, all or portions of 78 wetland basins occupy 108 ha of this land base. Based on NWI data, these basins are classified as lakes ($n = 4$), semipermanent wetlands ($n = 7$), seasonal wetlands ($n = 56$), and temporary wetlands ($n = 11$). However, aerial photography indicates that numerous smaller depressions were not mapped (GAK). Based on a historic survey conducted in 1917, common spikerush and tule bulrush were common in Florence Lake and sago pondweed and spike watermilfoil were abundant (Metcalf 1931). A current survey has not been conducted, but scattered small patches of bulrush were noted along the perimeter of some lakes, whereas spikerush, smartweed, and pondweed were noted in a small seasonal wetland during April 2004 (MKL).

The remainder of Florence Lake NWR consists of native (395 ha) and tame (82 ha) grass, woodland (6 ha), and crops (127 ha). Although approximately 82% of grasslands are often referred to as native, baseline vegetation monitoring indicate current species composition has been compromised to varying extents (Table 6). Sampling methodology was consistent with that of the belt transect data collected on Long Lake NWR in 2004 (Grant et al.

2004). Based on 50 belt transects ($n = 2500$ data points) established at varying locations on Florence NWR, the frequency of native and exotic vegetation occurrence along transects in 2002 was 7.0% and 93.0%, respectively. Further, these data indicate that 39.4% and 57.2% of the prairie has been moderately and heavily invaded by exotic plants, respectively (Table 6). Finally, farming has occurred periodically on Florence NWR since the early 1960s, but crop yields in recent years have been marginal. Thus, the cooperative farming agreement on 45 ha of fee title land was not renewed when it expired and these areas were seeded to grass in 2000. The current 127 ha of crops occur only on easements that are not controlled by the USFWS.

Wildlife Conservation

The primary purpose of NWR lands considered in this report is as a breeding ground for migratory birds and other wildlife; thus, any discussion regarding management in relation to long-term sustainability must be placed in this context. In addition, the 1997 NWRSIA mandates that each NWR develop a CCP consistent with the principles of sound fish and wildlife management and available science (Public Law 10557). The NWRSIA specifies that each CCP shall identify and describe the purposes of each NWR; the distribution, migration patterns, and abundance of fish, wildlife, and plant populations and related habitats; significant problems that may adversely affect the populations and habitats of fish, wildlife, and plants and the actions necessary to correct or mitigate such problems; and, to the maximum extent practicable and consistent with the NWRSIA, be consistent with fish and wildlife conservation plans of the state in which each NWR is located. Although important, the purpose of this report is not to fully develop information on all species potentially occurring on all three NWRs. However, some general future direction must be specified with regard to wildlife given the purpose for establishment of each NWR. Therefore, this report concentrates on the importance of all three NWRs for migratory birds because they represent a primary USFWS responsibility under requirements of the Migratory Bird Treaty Act of 1918 (16 U.S.C. § 715d). However, this focus should not be interpreted as meaning other vertebrates, invertebrates, and plants can be ignored because they are critical to proper system function. In addition to various metrics of biodiversity, lands of each NWR also contribute to other ecosystem services at various spatial scales, including floodwater storage, erosion control, and water quality. Thus, information regarding other natural resource values provided by each NWR also should be developed and integrated prior to evaluating the direction of future management.

Baseline information on the avian community of each NWR considered in this report was developed using a variety of data, including the 2002 version of the Long Lake NWR Bird List, which is periodically updated by Complex staff (URL http://longlake. fws.gov/birdlist.HTM). Naming conventions for all birds follows the American Ornithologists' Union Committee on Classification and Nomenclature (American Ornithologists' Union 1998, 2000, 2002, 2003). Several qualifying factors must be considered when considering this species list. First, the 26 accidental species documented on Long Lake NWR are not considered in this report. Second, the list is based on bird sightings over a long time period and it may not accurately represent the current avian community. Third, the list only reflects occurrence; thus, species populations on each NWR are not known. Regardless of these constraints, a list of avian species known to occur on at least one of the NWRs considered in this report can help focus discussion among individuals (e.g., USFWS personnel, core CCP team) responsible for determining the future management direction.

The NWRSIA states that national and regional plans must be consulted in developing a CCP. To provide overall perspective, relevant information regarding avian species of concern and population targets contained in a representative sample of these plans has been summarized (Appendix B), but no attempt has been made to prioritize or make decisions regarding species or guilds that should receive attention. In some cases, species considered to be of conservation concern at a regional level may not be of concern at a national level, or vice versa. Such differences do not indicate discrepancies; rather, they suggest differences in distribution and population status at different geographical scales. Also, some species mentioned in regional and national plans may not be incorporated in the table even though one or more of these three NWRs may potentially provide valuable resources for those species. The relatively small size of each NWR considered in this report precludes providing quality habitat for all species and decisions likely will be required to evaluate tradeoffs in management approaches and for development of detailed habitat objectives.

Long Lake NWR Complex. The importance of NWR lands (including the WMD) for waterbirds was a prime impetus for originally acquiring lands in fee title and also for subsequent expansion of the land base via fee title and easement acquisitions. Since 1987, the USFWS has conducted annual population surveys of 13 waterfowl species in each of 15 WMDs throughout the Dakotas and northeastern Montana. Information derived from this survey includes number of recruits, recruitment rates (i.e., the number of young females fledged per adult female in the breeding population), number of breeding pairs, number of wet ponds, and wet area. Of the 13 primary duck species breeding in the Prairie Pothole Region, the number of breeding pairs that used lands comprising the Long Lake Complex and surrounding private lands within the WMD ranged from 8865 in 1990 to 544,017 in 1997, whereas recruitment rates ranged from 0.40 in 1990 to 0.82 in 1997 (Table 7). According to the USFWS (1996), a minimum recruitment rate of 0.49 is needed to maintain a duck species' population. Additionally,

positive relationships between wetland condition (i.e., wet area, number of wet ponds) and both breeding pairs and duck recruitment can be seen throughout the 18-year survey period.

Information on nesting waterfowl is available from upland fields on six WPAs (156 ha) in the Long Lake WMD that were evaluated in 2001 and seven management units (168 ha) on Long Lake NWR evaluated in 2002 (GAK). Only fields dominated by perennial cover and supporting > 31 duck pairs per km^2 were selected for study on WPAs, whereas sites on Long Lake NWR were randomly selected. Vegetation composition of fields evaluated ranged from planted dense nesting cover, tame grass fields, and native grassland on WPAs to exotic cool season grass (e.g., Kentucky bluegrass, smooth brome) on Long Lake NWR. Nest density on WPA fields was approximately 0.76 per ha and Mayfield (Mayfield 1961) nest success ($n = 110$) of all species ($n = 7$) and study fields combined was 26.8%, which is greater than the 15.0% nest success generally accepted as the minimum for duck population stability in this region (Cowardin et al. 1985, Klett et al. 1988). However, Mayfield (Mayfield 1961) nest success of individual fields ranged from 4.2% to 38.8% (Table 8). Nest density on Long Lake NWR management units was approximately 1 per 2 ha and Mayfield (Mayfield 1961) nest success ($n = 79$) of all species ($n = 6$) and fields combined was only 3.0% (range among individual study fields = 0.4 to 17.8%; Table 8). The predominant nest predator on both the WPA fields and Long Lake NWR management units evaluated was the striped skunk; however nests also were predated by badger, raccoon, and red fox.

Excluding accidental species, the 2002 Long Lake NWR Bird List indicates that 278 species have been recorded on Long Lake NWR or private land in close proximity to the NWR, of which 129 have been documented as nesting. This diversity of bird life has resulted in national recognition of both Kidder County and Long Lake NWR as two of the top 10 birding "hot spots" in the nation (Konrad 1996). Long Lake NWR also is recognized as a Globally Important Bird Area (IBA) (URL http://www.abcbirds.org/iba/). The IBA program, initiated by BirdLife International in Europe in the mid-1980s, was developed to recognize and support sites of importance to birds (Kushlan et al. 2002).

Long Lake NWR was designated as a regional shorebird site in the Western Hemisphere Shorebird Reserve Network (WHSRN) in 2002 because more than 20,000 shorebirds use this NWR annually as either a migratory stopover or breeding area (URL http://www.manomet.org/WHSRN). From 2001 to 2004, shorebird surveys have been conducted on Long Lake NWR following Manomet Center for Conservation Sciences' International Shorebird Survey protocol. Although two survey routes have been established, most surveys have been conducted on the west route (comprised of the western 33% of Long Lake NWR). From 2001 - 2003, 28 shorebird species were recorded annually on Long Lake NWR, compared to 29 species in 2004. During this period, the most abundant spring migrants include Wilson's Phalarope and Marbled Godwit, whereas the most abundant fall migrants included Wilson's Phalarope, Long-billed and Short-billed dowitchers, American Avocets, and Killdeer. Both shorebird abundance and diversity has varied seasonally and annually throughout the survey period; abundance has ranged from 17,685 in spring 2004 to 1551 in spring 2003, whereas Simpson's Diversity Index (Simpson 1949) (range = 0.0 [low] to 1.0 [high]) values have varied from a seasonal low of 0.4978 to an annual high of 0.8218 (GAK). The substantial variation in shorebird abundance likely is related to wetland conditions at scales greater than Long Lake NWR. During years when numerous prairie wetlands are flooded and the water level in Long Lake is high (i.e., spring 2003), relatively few shorebirds use Long Lake NWR. Conversely, substantially more shorebirds use Long Lake NWR during years of minimal spring runoff (i.e., spring 2004) because the surrounding landscape is mostly dry and Long Lake provides suitable shorebird habitat.

Also during 2002, wetlands within the boundaries of Long Lake NWR and 10 WPAs (eight Bureau of Land Management transfer tracts) were designated as critical habitat for the federally threatened Piping Plover by the USFWS, Division of Ecological Services. Three fee title sites (Rath WPA, Rachel Hoff WPA, and Long Lake NWR) designated as Piping Plover critical habitat have been surveyed at five-year intervals, beginning in 1991, as part of the International Piping Plover Breeding Census (GAK). This is a complete census intended to provide moderate- and long-term information necessary to assess the success of Piping Plover recovery efforts and objectives (Ferland and Haig 2002). During the three survey years, 13 adults (six on Rachel Hoff WPA and seven on Long Lake NWR) were detected in 1991, five adults were detected on Rachel Hoff WPA in 1996, and seven adults (two on Rachel Hoff WPA and five on Long Lake NWR) and three young (all on Rachel Hoff WPA) were detected in 2001 (GAK).

The importance of the Long Lake NWR Complex to colonial nesting waterbirds has been investigated. In 2003, an aerial survey of all wetland basins ($n = 864$) on fee title lands within the Long Lake NWR Complex was completed and each wetland was assigned to one of three categories (high probability [HPC], moderate probability [MPC], and low probability [LPC]) based on the likelihood that the basin would support one or more waterbird colonies that year. Category assignments were based on a combination of habitat conditions, including (1) wetland cover type (Stewart and Kantrud 1971), (2) hydrologic regime and basin size (based on NWI data), and (3) special features (e.g., islands, dead trees in wetland). All of the HPC wetlands ($n = 68$) were ground surveyed for waterbird colonies, whereas 50% of the MPC wetlands ($n = 83$) and 5% of the LPC wetlands ($n = 32$) were ground surveyed. When a waterbird colony was located, species

composition was determined, nests were tallied, the perimeter of the colony was delineated using a global positioning system, and general habitat variables were measured.

Forty colonies were located during the survey, including 31 (77.5%) marsh colonies, eight (20%) ground or island colonies, and one (2.5%) tree or shrub colony. Twenty-four (60.0%) of the forty colonies consisted of only one species, 11 (27.5%) contained two species, three (7.5%) contained three species, one (2.5%) contained five species, and one (2.5%) contained eight species. Fourteen different breeding waterbird species were recorded, but only the Double-crested Cormorant utilized multiple colony types. The number of breeding pairs of each species detected during the survey ranged from three pairs of Snowy Egret to 310 pairs of California Gull (Table 9). Thirty-eight colonies (95%) were located on HPC wetlands, whereas only two (5%) colonies were located on MPC wetlands and no colonies were located on LPC wetlands (Table 9). The apparent success of the wetland stratification scheme provided a colonial nesting waterbird population estimate for NWR lands that had low variance and provided an accurate estimate of colonial nesting waterbird use of fee title lands during the 2003 breeding season.

Finally, the Complex staff has monitored the relative abundance and species composition of grassland/ wetland edge nesting passerines on Long Lake NWR at 50 randomly selected 100-m radius points annually from 2001 to 2004. Relative abundance (mean number of breeding pairs per point), estimated mean pairs per 100 ha, and frequency of occurrence (percentage of total points at which a species was detected) were calculated for all detected species (Table 10). The number of species detected annually ranged from 10 in 2002 to 14 in 2004 and the number of breeding pairs ranged from 258 in 2003 to 378 in 2004.

Bird Conservation Region. Lands of the Long Lake NWR Complex are in the Prairie Pothole Bird Conservation Region (BCR 11), an ecologically distinct region of 715,000 km2 with similar bird communities, habitats, and resource management issues (North American Bird Conservation Initiative, URL http://www.nabci-us.org/map. html). The Prairie Pothole BCR comprises the core breeding range of most dabbling duck and several diving duck species, as well as provides critical breeding and migration habitat for > 200 other bird species. There are 29 species of conservation concern listed for BCR 11 (USFWS 2002), all of which have been recorded as occurring on Long Lake NWR (Appendix B). Priority wetland species that breed in the area include Yellow Rail, Piping Plover, American Avocet, Marbled Godwit, Wilson's Phalarope, and Franklin's Gull. In addition, wetland areas in the region also provide important migration habitat for the American Golden-Plover, Hudsonian Godwit, White-rumped, and Buff-breasted sandpipers. Priority species that breed in terrestrial habitats include Sprague's Pipit, Baird's Sparrow, and Chestnut-collared Longspur (USFWS 2002).

Birds of Conservation Concern. The Birds of Conservation Concern (BCC) is the most recent effort to satisfy the 1988 amendment to the Fish and Wildlife Conservation Act, which mandates the USFWS to "…identify species, subspecies, and populations of all migratory nongame birds that, without additional conservation actions, are likely to become candidates for listing under the Endangered Species Act of 1973" (USFWS 2002). The document provides species lists at three geographic scales: national, USFWS regions, and BCRs. Species considered for inclusion include nongame birds, game birds without hunting seasons, and numerous categories (candidate, proposed endangered or threatened, and recently delisted) used in the Endangered Species Act. Parameters considered in determining if species within these categories are of concern include population size, extent of range, threats to habitat, and other factors. The BCC should be consulted for details regarding the assessment process (USFWS 2002).

Of the 278 bird species on the Long Lake NWR Complex Bird List, 49 are included in the BCC (Appendix B). Of these, 23 species are of concern at all three scales (i.e., BCR 11, Region 6 of the USFWS, National), three species (Prairie Falcon, American Golden-Plover, and Dickcissel) are of concern only at the Region 6 and National scales, one species (Short-eared Owl) is of concern only within BCR 11 and Region 6, and one species (Hudsonian Godwit) is of concern within BCR 11 and nationally, but not at a regional scale (Appendix B). The remaining species (n= 21) are of concern at only one scale (National = 15, USFWS Region 6 = 2, BCR = 4).

North American Waterfowl Management Plan. The national goals set forth in the 1998 update of the North American Waterfowl Management Plan (NAWMP) include: (1) maintaining the current diversity of duck species throughout North America and achieving a continental breeding population of 62 million ducks (mid-continent population of 39 million) during years with average environmental conditions, which would support a fall flight of 100 million, (2) reaching or exceeding mid-continent populations for 10 individual species, including Gadwall, American Wigeon, Mallard, Blue-winged and Cinnamon teal, Northern Shoveler, Northern Pintail, Green-winged Teal, Canvasback, Redhead, Greater and Lesser scaup, and (3) attaining an American Black Duck mid-winter population index of 385,000. The target populations for those species occurring on lands comprising the Long Lake NWR Complex are presented in Appendix B. The plan also establishes objectives for six goose species, three Trumpeter Swan populations, and two Tundra Swan populations. Of these, relevant objectives include reducing all five populations of Canada Geese that migrate through the central flyway and reducing mid-continent populations of

Snow and Greater White-fronted geese to 1,000,000 and 600,000, respectively. The plan also sets forth objectives to increase the interior population of Trumpeter Swans to 2500 and slightly reduce the eastern population of Tundra Swans to 80,000 (Appendix B). Finally, habitat objectives for the entire United States include protection of 2,856,785 ha, restoration of 1,249,352 ha, and enhancement of 2,922,126 ha (NAWMP, URL http://northamerican. fws.gov/NAWMP/images/update98.PDF).

Partners In Flight North American Landbird Conservation Plan. The North American Landbird Conservation Plan (NALCP) is a synthesis of priorities to guide national and international conservation actions of 448 native landbirds from 45 families that breed in the United States and Canada (Rich et al. 2004). Each species is assigned a score ranging from one (low vulnerability) to five (high vulnerability) for six factors (population size, breeding distribution, nonbreeding distribution, threats to breeding, threats to nonbreeding, and population trend) (Rich et al. 2004). In addition, a Stewardship List was developed based on avifaunal biomes in North America. These biomes were delineated using cluster analyses to identify groups of BCRs that share similar avifaunas. For each biome, Stewardship Species are those species that have a proportionately high percentage of their world population within a single region during either the breeding or wintering season. The lands comprising the Long Lake NWR Complex are in the Prairie Avifaunal Biome, which is composed of BCRs 11, 17 - 19, and 21 - 23. Almost 40% of the species on the Partners in Flight Watch List due to declining population trends or high threats occur in this biome (Rich et al. 2004, URL http://www.partnersinflight. org, URL http://www.rmbo.org/pif/pifdb.html).

The Watch List and Stewardship List of continentally important species in the United States and Canada currently include 100 and 158 species (66 species on the Stewardship List also occur on the Watch List), respectively (Rich et al. 2004). Within the Prairie Avifaunal Biome, there are 21 and seven species of continental importance on the Watch List and Stewardship List, respectively. Of these 28 species, 22 (Watch List = 16 species, Stewardship List = six species) have been recorded as occurring on the Long Lake NWR Complex (Appendix B). The recommended conservation action for three of these species is immediate action (Greater Prairie-Chicken, Baird's and Henslow's sparrows), whereas 11 species (Swainson's Hawk, Short-eared Owl, Red-headed Woodpecker, Willow Flycatcher, Sprague's Pipit, Lark Bunting, Grasshopper and Harris's sparrows, Chestnut-collared Longspur, Dickcissel, and Rusty Blackbird) require management and six species (Sharp-tailed Grouse, American Tree and Nelson's Sharp-tailed sparrows, and McCown's, Lapland, and Smith's longspurs) necessitate long-term planning and responsibility.

Shorebird Conservation Plan. The lands of the Long Lake NWR Complex are in the Northern Plains/Prairie Pothole Region (NP/PPR), an area that encompasses more than 810,666 km2 and includes all or portions of seven states and two BCRs (Prairie Potholes, Badland and Prairies) (Skagen and Thompson 2003). The landscape is characterized by rolling prairie interspersed with millions of depressional wetlands, intermittent and permanent streams and rivers, and agriculture. Thirty-six shorebird species occur in the NP/PPR, 35 of which have been observed on or adjacent to Long Lake NWR. Of the 13 species known to breed in the region, nine species (Piping Plover, Killdeer, American Avocet, Willet, Spotted and Upland sandpipers, Marbled Godwit, Wilson's Snipe, and Wilson's Phalarope) have been documented as nesting on Long Lake NWR and five of these species (Piping Plover, American Avocet, Upland Sandpiper, Marbled Godwit, and Wilson's Phalarope) are listed as species of regional concern (Appendix B). The Piping Plover also is listed as threatened under the Endangered Species Act. The NP/PPR also is a major migration route for western hemispheric shorebirds. In addition, the NP/PPR is considered particularly important for 10 migrant shorebirds (American Golden-Plover, Semipalmated Plover, Lesser Yellowlegs, Semipalmated, White-rumped, Baird's, and Pectoral sandpipers, Dunlin, Stilt Sandpiper, and Long-billed Dowitcher). Although none of these species is considered a regional species of concern, the provision of adequate stopover habitat is a regional priority. Nearly 27% of small shorebirds (total body length < 190 mm in the mid-continent region migrate through the NP/PPR in spring, whereas > 22% of medium-sized shorebirds utilize the NP/PPR during fall migration (Appendix B; Skagen and Thompson 2003; U.S. Shorebird Conservation Plan, URL http://shorebirdplan.fws.gov/RegionalShorebird/downloads/NORPLPP2.doc).

Waterbird Conservation Region. The lands of the Long Lake NWR Complex are located in the Northern Prairie and Parkland Region (NPPR) of the North American Waterbird Conservation Plan (NAWCP). The boundaries of the NPPR occur in two disjunctive areas that include four Canadian provinces and five states in the U.S. The NPPR boundary is similar to the BCR 11 boundary, but also includes portions of BCRs 6 and 10. The NPPR also overlaps areas covered by the Prairie Habitat Joint Venture in Canada and the Prairie Pothole Joint Venture (PPJV) in the U.S.

The NAWCP focuses on members of eight orders and 22 families of birds, including coastal waterbirds, wading birds, and marshbirds (Waterbird Conservation for the Americas, URL http://www.waterbirdconservation.org/waterbirds/). There are 71 species of waterbirds that occur in the NPPR; 24 colonial and 15 non-colonial species that breed, and an additional 32 species that occur as migrants or winter visitors. Of these 71 species, 59 species (33 breeding, 7 regular migrants, and 19 casual species) occur in North Dakota. Twenty of the 33 breeding species and one (Whooping Crane) of seven regular migrant species that occur in North Dakota have been documented on the Long Lake NWR (Appendix B). The conservation status of the 20 breeding species at Long Lake NWR includes six that are of high concern (Horned and Western grebes, American Bittern, Yellow Rail, Franklin's Gull, and Black Tern), four of moderate concern (Eared Grebe, Black-crowned Night-Heron, Virginia Rail, and Common Tern) and 10 species considered low risk (Beyersbergen et al. 2004, URL http://birds.fws.gov/waterbirds/NPP/). Although not documented as current breeders, Long Lake NWR has documented the occurrence of two species (Whooping Crane and Least Tern) that are listed for protection under the Endangered Species Act.

Prairie Pothole Joint Venture. The lands comprising the Long Lake NWR Complex are within the boundaries of the PPJV of the NAWMP. Joint ventures were originally conceived by the USFWS in 1986 to implement the NAWMP. Established in 1989, the goal of the PPJV is to increase waterfowl populations through habitat conservation projects that improve natural diversity (diversity defined as an appropriate mix of plant and animal communities that can be sustained in association with profitable agriculture). However, in addition to waterfowl, many joint ventures (including the PPJV) are now incorporating an "all bird" approach. There are 225 species that breed in the PPR, including several grassland species (e.g., Lark Bunting, Grasshopper and Baird's sparrows, Dickcissel, and Bobolink) that have declined significantly over the past three decades (U.S. Prairie Pothole Joint Venture 1995). The objectives established for the PPJV include (1) conserve habitat capable of supporting 6.8 million breeding ducks by the year 2001 and (2) stabilize or increase populations of declining wetland and grassland-associated wildlife species in the PPR, with special emphasis on non-waterfowl migratory birds (U.S. Prairie Pothole Joint Venture 1995). Habitat objectives in the PPR include protection of 765,486 ha, restoration of 301,456 ha, and enhancement of 1,485,026 ha (URL http://northamerican.fws.gov/NAWMP/images/update98.PDF).

Biological Assessment

Approach

The USFWS is involved in the management of more than 607,000 ha in North Dakota (Byersbergen et al. 2004). However, many of these areas are small and embedded within a larger landscape that has been greatly modified by past land uses and management. In North Dakota, agriculture represents the primary land use, and one consequence of this modification has been the fragmentation of the prairie landscape into smaller parcels that has negatively impacted many regional and local faunal communities (Samson 1980, Johnson and Temple 1986, Knopf and Samson 1995). For example, 55 species from the Great Plains currently are listed as threatened or endangered, and an additional 728 species represent potential additions to this list (Flores 1995). In addition to biodiversity, however, other important natural resource challenges also are emerging. Past and current land uses have negatively impacted air and water quality, water availability, floodwater storage, and a host of other ecosystem services (Huntzinger 1995, Krupa and Legge 1995). Although often portrayed as separate entities, these values are interrelated and all are determined by ecosystem processes. For example, the planting of non-native vegetation to reduce soil erosion and improve water quality also directly influences habitat suitability for different fauna. Therefore, prior to implementing management actions, a comprehensive evaluation of potential changes to current ecosystem processes must be undertaken to fully understand the implications of different strategies. This is particularly important today because an increasingly diverse group of stakeholders with different attitudes and desires are participating in natural resource management decision making. This does not imply that all ecosystem services must be provided on a single NWR; rather, it suggests pertinent information on all aspects of ecosystem services be evaluated to maximize the probability that stakeholders with different backgrounds and interests understand the full range of potential trade-offs. For example, a primary purpose of the Long Lake NWR Complex is the provision of habitat for migratory birds and other wildlife. However, the NWRSIA (and internal USFWS guidance documents and policies) also stresses the importance of biotic integrity and ecosystem health. Thus, the impact of planned management actions on these components, as well as those valued by other agencies and private landowners, should be considered.

Understanding processes should be a key factor in natural resource management decisions. This can only be accomplished by also considering the formation and historical context of landscapes (Jensen et al. 1996, Swanson et al. 1988) because the success of management actions is constrained by the properties of the land being managed. This is particularly true in the Great Plains because the environment is easy to alter, yet can collapse quickly (Flores 1995). The authors have termed this perspective the concept of "ecological fit" and defined it as follows: the idea that the health and sustainability of ecosystems depends on how well management acts are coordinated with acts of nature. The principal tenets of this concept are (1) ecosystem function depends on synergistic processes involving both uplands and wetlands, (2) a given land unit (e.g., wetland basin) can undergo dramatic changes in structure and function in relation to short- and long-term acts of nature, and (3) processes are interrelated; thus, any action intended to alter a specific function may have unintended results.

The following evaluation is based on the tenets of ecological fit. However, Slade and Florence Lake NWRs were not investigated in detail during the site visit and little relevant information can be provided regarding the current condition of system function and structure. Thus, information gleaned from the few sites visited on Slade and Florence Lake NWRs is used throughout the remainder of this document to draw comparisons with Long Lake NWR.

A review of records for each NWR revealed that much information pertaining to the results of past management actions has been recorded, but details regarding impacts to abiotic factors (e.g., soils, water quality) often are lacking or incomplete. Thus, it is not possible to arrive at definitive conclusions regarding how past management actions have altered the systems encompassing each of the NWRs. This is not surprising given that the importance of these factors to management is only beginning to be understood and applied. Therefore, general information contained in the literature, in combination with information provided Complex staff, is used to identify potential challenges that the planning team should consider when developing the CCP. The intent is not to advocate an attempt to return the land to pre-European settlement conditions. This is unrealistic given the many perturbations to the system. Rather, the intent is to transfer information necessary to develop an understanding of current system function for the purpose of assisting the Complex staff in the development of a management program that will achieve the goals of the Long Lake NWR Complex, adjacent landowners, and society for productive and sustainable natural resource benefits.

Current Conditions

Hydrology. Historically, Long Lake was part of the ancestral Cannonball River. Fine materials (clays and silts) transported by glacial meltwater settled in areas of diminished flow velocities resulting in areas with relatively impervious soils that stored large quantities of water. In many cases (e.g., Long Lake), these areas were sited in topographically low areas and functioned to capture some water transported through the valley. Following glacial retreat and subsequent warming, obstructions (e.g., ice dams) blocking valleys disappeared and water in the fluvial system encompassing Long Lake was transported through a network of channels to the Missouri River. However, topographically low areas such as Long Lake remained and accumulated water periodically. The primary hydrologic input was surface water (e.g., precipitation, runoff), but ground water movement through adjacent terraces also influenced lake hydrology and chemistry. Although speculative, during years of low total inflow, surface water likely was not discharged from these sites and was lost only by evaporation and transpiration. In years of high inflows, however, surface waters increased above a natural sill and water was discharged downstream. The variable surface water inputs that occurred seasonally and annually, in combination with topography (elevation ranges from 521.2 to 523.0 m above mean sea level [msl]) and ground-water chemistry, resulted in Long Lake being a relatively shallow, alkaline lake that exhibited dynamic water-level fluctuations.

Although the valley encompassing Long Lake NWR retains many historic features, the area has been modified by both on-going natural processes and anthropogenic forces. Perhaps the greatest change that has impacted Long Lake NWR is hydrologic alteration. Surface water, which enters Long Lake via Long Lake Creek (~68%) and runoff from surrounding uplands (~32%), remains the primary hydrologic input to Long Lake and water is still discharged from Long Lake to the Missouri River via Apple Creek when surface water exceeds a certain threshold. However, dike construction and altered land-use patterns in the watershed likely have altered the quantity, timing, and frequency of water inflows and outflows. Limited information documenting hydrologic alterations was located for the watershed; thus, only information for Long Lake NWR improvements obtained from staff is provided. Following purchase in the 1930s, the USFWS estimated that the natural outlet of Long Lake was 522.2 m above msl. During 1936 and 1937, the Civilian Conservation Corps (CCC) constructed three dikes (denoted as A, B, and C) across Long Lake to form three units and built several small dams to trap water in coulees entering Long Lake. Several modifications to the lake dikes (e.g., increased height and addition of water control structures and spillways) were made during the 1940s, but two of the dikes (B and C) washed out in 1950. In 1954, all three dikes were rebuilt to an elevation of 524.3 m above msl and equipped with spillways. The spillway in A Dike located at the west end of Unit 1 was constructed at an elevation of 523.0 m above msl, whereas the spillways in B Dike (separating Unit 1 and Unit 2) and C Dike (separating Unit 2 and Unit 3) were constructed at an elevation of 523.2 m above msl (GAK). Since 1950, additional dikes have been constructed adjacent to Long Lake to capture surface water that enters from natural drainage paths originating in the uplands. In many cases (e.g., Unit 2 Marsh), these impoundments can be flooded either by natural runoff or by transporting water from Long Lake via gravity flow, but dewatering is dependent on evapotranspiration. Currently, the staff can manage water in seven impoundments (three units of Long Lake and four impoundments) on Long Lake NWR.

The specific hydrologic impacts of dike construction are difficult to determine due to limited on-site information. However, the construction of dikes across the lake obstructed water movement within the original lake bed. Lake bathymetry data were not located, but observation suggests the dikes were constructed across the natural elevation gradient. Thus, the pattern and timing of flooding in different portions of Long Lake was altered because water from Long Lake Creek was sequentially impounded behind each dike until a sufficient volume accumulated to discharge water over the spillway into the next unit. In contrast, the historic flooding pattern was determined by natural elevation gradients throughout the entire lake basin (e.g., water entering Long Lake pooled first in lowest areas throughout the basin). Second, spillways were constructed to heights greater than two feet above the elevation of the historic lake outlet. Therefore, the potential depth of flooding was increased.

Available inflow records indicate Long Lake Creek is a perennial stream that exhibits sporadic flows. Thus, although the creek represents a reliable source of water, the volume of water is not predictable. For example, no water was discharged over the spillway in A Dike in 13 of 25 years between 1963 and 1987 (GAK). During this period, inflows from Long Lake Creek ranged from 895 to 5836 ha-m (average = 2253 ha-m). In contrast, during years when water was discharged over A Dike, inflows ranged from 1862 to 12,506 ha-m (average = 6235 ha-m). Coupled with the requirement to flood units sequentially, these data, although imprecise, suggest land comprising Unit 1 is flooded more frequently and to a greater extent than would occur naturally, whereas some land comprising Unit 3 is flooded less frequently and for shorter time periods compared to historic conditions. For example, Unit 3 was dry by mid-August in six of the 13 years that no water was discharged over the spillway in A Dike. During this period, the surface flooding recorded in Unit

3 likely resulted from discharge of surface water from several large coulees that drain surrounding uplands and discharge directly into Units 2 and 3. The amount of water entering each unit is not known, but staff estimated that Long Lake Creek represented only 68% of the surface water input. If correct, the remaining 32% of runoff originates from other sources such as coulees that drain surrounding uplands and discharge directly into each unit. In some years, this input could be substantial. For example, during the period 1963 to 1986, annual precipitation recorded at Long Lake NWR ranged from 23.6 to 55.9 cm and averaged 40.8 cm during years when water was not discharged over the spillway in A Dike. However, this information does not adequately represent current inputs because additional dikes have been constructed across some of these coulees since 1986 (e.g., Unit 2 Marsh completed in 1987). Thus, the amount of surface inflows to Long Lake via these drainage paths has likely been reduced.

In general, all dikes on Long Lake NWR were installed to improve water management flexibility. However, a primary purpose for separating Long Lake into units was to better manage water to prevent botulism outbreaks (USFWS 1988). Thus, many of the aforementioned hydrologic alterations caused by dikes were intentional. For example, the goal of water management from 1944 to 1959 was to fill Unit 1 to 523.0 m, Unit 2 to 522.9 m, and Unit 3 to 522.7 m above msl. This strategy was considered highly effective for Units 1 and 2, but Unit 3 could not reliably be stabilized and frequently went dry. Between 1960 and 1987, the water management strategy basically remained the same for Units 1 and 2, but Unit 3 was maintained in as dry a condition as possible. Although Unit 3 was dry nine of these 28 years, records indicate that the water management capability was inadequate to reliably meet these goals (USFWS 1988), which indicates that natural climate cycles still influenced water-level fluctuations to some extent. The current strategy is based on water elevations in the spring; if water levels do not exceed a certain threshold (522.9 m msl), Unit 3 is kept as dry as possible; otherwise Unit 3 is flooded to the extent possible.

The success of these water management strategies in reducing botulism outbreaks is difficult to interpret. Prior to initiating water management in 1944, the estimated total avian deaths from botulism between 1937 and 1943 exceeded 375,000 and ranged from 75 in 1938 to 145,000 in 1941 (Figure 2). In contrast, the total estimated loss between 1944 and 2004 was only 82,953 birds (range = 0 to 18,700) (McEnroe 1986, USFWS 1988, USFWS unpublished data). This suggests that developing the ability to control water levels provided some ability to ameliorate the incidence and extent of botulism outbreaks. However, numerous factors are involved in the progression from the initiation and propagation phases to large botulism outbreaks (Wobeser 1997). Further, there are likely many alternative pathways that lead to an outbreak;

thus, determining effective management practices is hampered by an incomplete knowledge of the environmental factors that precipitate outbreaks (Wobeser and Bollinger 2002). In general, it has been recommended that control efforts need to focus on three important factors: (1) fluctuating water levels during hot summer months, (2) an abundance of flies, and (3) presence of animal carcasses necessary for toxin production (Lock and Friend 1989). Thus, although it is plausible that water management contributed to prevention, other factors likely were involved as well. For example, factors reported as potentially signifying an increased risk of a botulism outbreak include increasing temperature, increasing invertebrate abundance or biomass, and decreasing turbidity (Rocke et al. 1999). Unfortunately, data on botulism deaths and environmental factors for each individual unit were not located; thus, any conclusions regarding the effects of water management would be extremely speculative.

Sediment and Nutrient Dynamics. Regardless of how effective water management strategies have been with respect to controlling the incidence and extent of botulism outbreaks, human perturbations have likely impacted other processes that determine system structure and function, including the interrelated factors of sediment dynamics and nutrient loads. These factors are important because they affect both upland and wetland plant community dynamics. Inorganic nutrients provide the chemical constituents that form the basis of the entire food chain. Common nutrients needed in large quantities for cell development include oxygen, carbon, phosphorous, silica, sulfur, iron, magnesium, calcium, potassium, nitrogen, and hydrogen, whereas manganese, molybdenum, copper, zinc, and cobalt are minor nutrients that may occasionally be in short supply (Salisbury and Ross 1978, Goldman and Horne 1983, Table 11). Ionic compounds (e.g., sodium, potassium, and chloride) affect ion exchange at the surface of cell membranes, whereas toxic compounds can negatively impact nutrient cycling by causing mortality of plants or animals. Some inorganic compounds (e.g., copper and zinc) can act either as toxicants or as growth stimulators. In contrast, organic compounds tend to occur in small quantities in natural systems and some (e.g., humic acids and citrate) can alter the chemical state of water by changing the ionic state of metals that might otherwise be toxic.

The primary factors determining daily, seasonal, and long-term cycles of major elements in natural systems are rainfall, evaporation, erosion and solution, sedimentation, and biological components of the watershed (Goldman and Horne 1983). These factors, in turn, are influenced by parent material, climate, topography, and vegetation cover in the watershed. The extent that human perturbations have altered sediment dynamics and nutrient loads on each NWR cannot be determined directly because records are lacking or sporadic. However, soil organic matter greatly influences productivity by functioning as a binding agent that aids soil structure formation and stability, which is critical to maintaining adequate water infiltration and potential water storage (Peterson and Cole 1995). In addition, organic matter also is a primary requisite for retaining certain nutrients, particularly nitrogen. Therefore, loss of surface horizons in terrestrial habitats reduces nitrogen availability and, if sufficient losses occur, results in reduced plant productivity (Peterson and Cole 1995). Thus, concerns associated with past and current agricultural practices are not limited only to the fragmentation and loss of native vegetation that reduces habitat suitability for native wildlife. Rather, these activities also can accelerate soil erosion that can reduce the potential productivity of sites suffering soil loss, as well as negatively impact sites receiving increased sediment overburden (Kothmann 1995).

The extent that soil erosion and nutrient redistribution has occurred on lands encompassed by all three NWRs is unknown. However, 87% of improved prairie farmlands in the Great Plains are characterized as exhibiting medium to high erosion risk (Sopuck 1995) and the estimated average annual sheet and rill erosion on non-federal rural land for North Dakota in 1987 was 0.8 tons per ha in cropland, 0.2 tons per ha in pastureland, and 0.4 tons per ha in rangeland, whereas the estimated average annual wind erosion on cultivated and non-cultivated cropland was 1.7 tons per ha and 0.08 tons per ha, respectively (Kothmann 1995). Thus, it is likely that some soil erosion has occurred, particularly in areas with steeper slopes that have a history of cropping. In contrast, erosion is of less concern in areas of lesser impact. We provide two examples to illustrate this point. The first is from soil cores collected at Florence Lake NWR in an area that has been minimally impacted by past land uses. A core collected in a seasonal wetland suggested the presence of a deep A horizon on the surface and an argillic B horizon at about 16 in (40.6 cm). Further, soils were not mixed and exhibited a structure characteristic of a relatively unaltered wetland substrate. A second core collected at the top of a hill adjacent to this wetland also exhibited a well developed A horizon to a depth of 12.7 to 15.2 cm and an underlying B horizon, suggesting minimal soil erosion has occurred.

The other example is from soil cores collected in Unit G7 and Unit 2 Marsh of Long Lake NWR. Based on the county soil survey, soils in Unit G7 exhibit a sand mantle and a past land use history that may have included farming. The soil core collected near a knoll in this unit indicated that soil structure was generally lacking. The top 10 cm contained little organic material and was assumed to represent the A horizon and the underlying B horizon (10 - 20 cm) contained a mix of sand with small amounts of clay. The second core collected at the toe-slope of the same hill also indicated minimal soil structure, but the A horizon was at least 20 cm in depth and contained substantially more organic matter. Although not definitive, these two cores suggest that soil from the slopes has been transported (i.e., eroded) to surrounding low areas.

In conventional agriculture, the solution to soil degradation has consisted of using biological and chemical inputs (e.g., fertilizers) to replace nutrient losses (Sopuck 1995) and planting crop varieties adapted for growth under altered conditions. However, this complement of options often is not available when attempting to restore native prairie vegetation. First, the term native refers to plants that originally occupied the site of interest; thus planting new "varieties" is not plausible even if they were available. Second, unlike crop monocultures, mixed-grass prairie consists of numerous grass and forb species that exhibit a non-random distribution determined by abiotic factors (e.g., soil topography, climate). Therefore, application of fertilizer will not overcome the problems associated with the differential loss of organic matter. Finally, frequent cultivation to control introduced tame grasses and invasive plants cannot be performed simultaneously with the reestablishment of native grasses and forbs without causing mortality of desirable species.

In contrast to terrestrial sites, primary productivity of many disturbed wetlands often is reduced due to the excessive accumulation of sediments and nutrients (Rybicki and Carter 1986, Dieter 1991, Hartleb et al. 1993, Jurik et al. 1994, Wang et al. 1994, Gleason and Euliss 1998, Gleason et al. 2003). In terms of quantity, sediment has become the major pollutant of wetlands, lakes, estuaries, and reservoirs in the United States (Baker 1992) and many river systems are now considered degraded (Longcore et al. 1987, Grue et al. 1989). The greatest causes of altered water chemistry are contamination from agriculture, road construction, and industry (Ulrich and Pfeifer 1976, Swanson et al. 1988, Euliss et al. 1999) because these activities can alter the distribution of soils and sediments, which can act as both a sink and source for water quality constituents. In some cases, productivity can be affected by an imbalance in a single element. For example, salinity can directly inhibit germination and growth of plants (Swanson et al. 1988, Kantrud et al. 1989) and excessive additions of phosphorous (e.g., fertilizer runoff) can lead to extensive algal blooms that inhibit growth of some submerged aquatic plants (Robel 1961, Kullberg 1974, Swanson et al. 1988). In other situations, however, water-borne elements can act alone or synergistically to affect productivity. For example, salinity can exacerbate boron toxicity in several plant species (Wimmer et al. 2003). Further, suppression of primary production often negatively impacts secondary productivity. For example, salinity can influence invertebrate composition directly by affecting physiology (Newcombe and MacDonald 1991, Euliss et al. 1999) or indirectly by affecting habitat structure and foods (Krull, 1970, Wollheim and Lovvorn 1996). Other examples include documented reports that high concentrations of suspended silt and clay are toxic to zooplankton (Newcombe and MacDonald 1991) and agrichemicals can cause significant mortality of aquatic invertebrates (Borthwick 1988).

As mentioned previously, natural systems exhibit plasticity to fluctuations in water quality and sediments. For example, natural concentrations of dissolved solids within a single closed-basin wetland can fluctuate from fresh to extremely saline depending on climatic variables that influence hydrology (Swanson et al. 1988, LaBaugh 1989). Historically, the water chemistry of Long Lake likely was dynamic given that it was part of a riverine system characterized by sporadic flows that resulted in fluctuating lake levels. Intact upland and floodplain vegetation attenuated surface runoff and soil erosion, and acted as a filter to limit the amount of sediment that entered the creek channel and surrounding coulees. During periods of extended low flow, the volume of water entering Long Lake in some years was insufficient to overtop the natural outlet (elevation = 522.2 m); thus, Long Lake represented a terminal point of water collection. When this occurred, discharge of water downstream of Long Lake did not occur and water loss occurred only by evapotranspiration. This would tend to cause an increase in the concentration of organic and inorganic compounds. In contrast, during years of higher flow, the volume of water entering Long Lake would be sufficient to breach the natural outlet and water would be discharged downstream. During these periods, the concentration of organic and inorganic compounds in surface waters of Long Lake would decrease due to dilution and transport downstream. Unfortunately, data from USGS gauge stations above and below Long Lake are only available for a brief period in the late 1980s and early 1990s; therefore, it is not possible to evaluate the frequency with which these two extremes occurred. Nonetheless, the concentration of nutrients and elements in the waters of Long Lake likely was dynamic because variable surface water inputs resulted in the occasional concentration and dilution of nutrients and other elements as the region experienced climate extremes ranging from drought to deluge.

However, alterations that affect fundamental processes (e.g., hydrology, water chemistry, sediment dynamics) often alter system tolerance and can result in significant shifts in plant and invertebrate communities. River systems are concentration points for sediments and chemical constituents bound to sediments because they collect runoff from surrounding uplands. Thus, sediment transport and deposition is a naturally occurring process that affects formation, structure, and function of wetlands (Saucier 1994). Prior to human alteration, areas of transport and deposition tended to change temporally in response to channel characteristics that influenced flow velocities. Long Lake likely represented an area of accumulation within the watershed, but dynamic flow patterns resulted in periods of concentration and dilution. Further, the amount of sediment and bound constituents entering the system was within normal bounds and excess nutrients (e.g., nitrogen and phosphorus) could be processed without risk to long-term productivity. For example, wetlands may be capable of removing 70 to 90% of nitrogen entering a system (Gilliam 1994) and 20 to 100% of metals, depending on wetland type, individual site characteristics, and metal type (Taylor et al. 1990, Gambrell 1994). However, construction of dikes within the floodplain on Long Lake has likely contributed to altered sediment and chemical deposition patterns by changing flow velocities and other hydrologic parameters, including the frequency, depth, and time of flooding. Further, the type of alteration differs depending on the location of one dike relative to other dikes. For example, the upstream unit (Unit 1) likely receives a greater volume of water annually and discharge over the spillway occurs more frequently compared to the dike separating Unit 2 from Unit 3. As a result, the frequency of flushing flows likely decreases sequentially from Unit 1 to Unit 3. Coupled with potential increases in the amount of material entering the system, it is possible that sediment loads and concentrations of certain constituents vary within each unit.

Information on the rate of sediment accretion in wetlands was not located, but Complex staff indicated that palustrine wetlands surrounded by croplands likely have accrued sediment. During the site visit, soils inspected in a seasonal wetland on Slade NWR and in Unit 2 Marsh on Long Lake NWR also suggested that sediment accrual has occurred and turbid conditions in the Long Lake units suggested the presence of some unconsolidated sediments. In addition, a few historic records were located that compared water chemistry on either side of a single dike on Long Lake. In 1969, the chemistry on the east side of an unspecified road exhibited greater total alkalinity and specific conductivity and increased concentrations of sulfate chloride sodium, and potassium compared to the water on the west side of the same road (Swanson et al. 1988). Similar observations were recorded during the site visit; the specific conductivity of water in Units 1, 2, and 3 exhibited increasing values of 1910, 2600, and 4200 μS per cm, respectively. Although these limited data suggest changes in sediment dynamics and water chemistry, it is not possible to determine the extent that these observed differences are due to natural variation in climate (LaBaugh and Swanson 2004) as opposed to long-term changes resulting from dike construction and altered land use patterns.

Information also is lacking to quantify the extent that human influences have altered dynamic fluctuation of nutrients (e.g., nitrogen, phosphorous) and other elements (e.g., mercury, boron, arsenic) in the Long Lake Units. However, relative to historic conditions, management actions have increased water storage volumes up to three feet above the natural sill in the three Units. Retaining more water in the Units than would occur naturally, in combination with altering the frequency of flushing flows, will increase the overall potential for accumulation of various ions, elements, and other dissolved solids via evaporative processes. This potential can be demonstrated by using information on specific conductance and estimates of average annual lake evaporation. For example, total dissolved matter can be estimated from specific conductance data by multiplying by an empirical factor that typically varies from 0.5 to 1.0 (Figure 3). Ideally, the relationship between specific conductance and total dissolved matter is determined for a particular location. However, since this information is lacking, we used the factor 0.65 suggested by Rainwater and Thatcher (1960) because it provides a good approximation of total dissolved matter data presented in Table 3. Using this factor, estimates of total dissolved matter were within 3% (range = 1 to 6%) of those reported in Table 3. Given this relationship, each ha-m of water with a specific conductance of 1000 μS per cm that was stored and evaporated would result in the accumulation of 7.33 tons of total dissolved matter. When extrapolated to the area of each Unit (Unit 1 = 507.5 ha, Unit 2 = 827.6 ha, and Unit 3 = 5369.2 ha), the evaporation of 30.5 cm of water from all Units combined would result in the accumulation of 14,987.8 tons of dissolved matter (e.g., 6704 ha * 7.33 tons * 0.305). However, the amount of dissolve matter actually accumulated in each Unit will vary depending on evaporation rates (Figure 4). Given that the average annual lake evaporation for this region can exceed 91 cm (Shjeflo 1968), the above estimate is considered conservative.

Based on this simple example, it is reasonable to assume that management actions have promoted the concentration of evaporates in the Units. The effects of concentrating various chemical constituents (e.g., nitrogen, phosphorous, arsenic, boron, mercury) on biotic communities currently is unknown; however, it is reasonable to assume that in the near future certain biological thresholds may be breached that will cause a cascading collapse of the wetland ecosystem. As indicated earlier in this section, accumulation of various salts and other elements (e.g., boron) can be toxic to plants and cause osmotic regulation problems for a variety of species. An extensive review of the literature may provide the information necessary to make inferences about the various potential impacts of concentrating chemical constituents; however, it would be equally important to initiate a monitoring program to quantify exports and imports of water and associated chemical constituents in the wetland Units. For example, detailed information on pool elevations and the frequency, volume, and quality of water passing through the NWR could be used to better predict the accumulation rate of various chemical constituents in the Units. Moreover, this baseline information is necessary to evaluate the effectiveness of any future management actions implemented to change concentration trajectories (e.g., flushing flows).

Vegetation and Wildlife. The impacts of altered hydrology, soils, sediment dynamics, and nutrient distribution described above can have significant effects on both primary and secondary productivity. Thus, overall productivity in both the short- and long-term could be negatively impacted because plant community structure and composition influences use by invertebrates and vertebrates (Laubhan and Roelle 2001), whereas both plants and invertebrates play significant roles in nutrient cycling and are integral components in the food chains of a wide variety of vertebrates (Murkin and Batt 1987, Laubhan et al. 2005). Several graphs of avian habitat requirements were compiled from published literature to illustrate these relationships (Appendix C). Although this information may assist the Complex staff in establishing target habitat objectives, it is of little assistance in selecting appropriate management strategies or gauging the ability to achieve objectives. These latter challenges are critical to successful management and require understanding current system processes. For example, terrestrial vegetation on Slade NWR is dominated by tame grasses, whereas Florence Lake NWR retains more of a native component. Thus, existing information on species-habitat relationships could be used to predict potential shifts in avian community composition that would result from restoring a tame grass field to native vegetation on each NWR. However, the most appropriate strategy, or combination of strategies, to implement may differ among fields due to differences in current soil properties and other factors. Unfortunately, site-specific information regarding changes in abiotic factors (e.g., hydrology, soils, nutrients) and biotic factors (e.g., plant and invertebrate community composition and biomass) in response to land management activities is not available for Long Lake NWR. Therefore, it is not possible to determine the extent to which changes have occurred, nor is it possible to separate changes that are the result of natural variation from changes that are the result of human intervention. Consequently, it is not possible to identify causative mechanisms or derive conclusions regarding the value of different management strategies. Rather, the authors can only allude to potential changes that have occurred and offer our best professional judgment regarding the implications of these changes. For example, the two soil cores collected in Unit G7 showed signs that the surface horizons had been redistributed (see above). In 2000, this area was interseeded with native grasses, including sideoats and blue grama, big and little bluestem, prairie sandreed, western wheatgrass, green needle, and switchgrass. During the site visit, residual cover of both grama species, little bluestem, junegrass, purple prairie clover, white and fringed sage, Kentucky bluegrass, and smooth brome were noted during the brief examination of the hillslope and knoll. In contrast, Kentucky bluegrass and smooth brome dominated the toeslope. The failure of at least some plant species to become established is not uncommon on many restoration sites and, in many cases, may be due to altered moisture and nutrient retention properties of soils. Thus, using the concept of ecological fit, one approach to restoration would consist of seeding only those species that are adapted for germination and growth under existing soil conditions. This would require an initial cost of conducting soil surveys to document soil properties (e.g., presence/absence of A horizon, organic matter content, etc.) prior to initiating restoration, but the overall cost:benefit ratio may be favorable given that the likelihood of success would increase.

A second example involves the wetland plant community in the Long Lake units. The presence of annual and perennial vegetation (kochia, saltgrass, seepweed, bulrush, common reed, dock, smartweed) in Unit 2 Marsh and the seasonal wetlands on Slade and Florence Lake NWRs suggests that the sediment accretion observed during the site visit and any potential changes in water chemistry have not been sufficient to preclude vegetation establishment. However, this could be deceiving because sampling was neither rigorous nor comprehensive. Similarly, it is reasonable to assume that some changes in water chemistry have occurred in Long Lake throughout its history. For example, elevated levels of boron and mercury have been detected (Olson and Welsh 1991) and it is reasonable to assume that the salinity regime has been altered given that salinity is largely determined by hydrological processes (Euliss et al. 1999). During the site visit, emergent and submergent vegetation appeared to be scant in the flooded portions of the units, suggesting that resources (e.g., food, cover) available for waterbirds are at least temporarily reduced. However, insufficient information is available to determine if this change is related to natural events (e.g., wet/dry cycles), subtle yet significant changes in wetland processes (e.g., water chemistry) resulting from past management, or a combination of both factors. Obtaining the baseline information necessary to separate the influence of natural events from management actions may prove beneficial to ensuring the long-term sustainable productivity of wetlands on the Long Lake NWR Complex. Again, based on the concept of ecological fit, one approach to future management would consist of initiating monitoring programs to track fundamental ecological factors (e.g., water quality) that influence factors (e.g., plant germination and growth) higher in the trophic system. This would require additional equipment and staff time, but such information would provide the means to identify future issues sufficiently early to allow corrective management actions to be implemented when effectiveness is greatest and costs are reduced.

Potential Information Needs

The site visit concentrated primarily on Long Lake NWR and discussions focused on three interrelated issues: hydrology, soils/sediments, and nutrients/water chemistry. Based on the authors' experiences, these factors are among the most common issues that effect management potential and success. However, little baseline information exists and quantifying changes often are impossible because site-specific information is required. In contrast, the Complex staff has collected substantially more information on vertebrate populations and recently started collecting baseline information on terrestrial plant communities. Coupled with existing information in the literature (e.g., Appendix C), this information will prove valuable in the near future, particularly if it can be interpreted relative to system processes. Unfortunately, the authors' attempts to locate relevant information on processes were only marginally successful. Thus, it appears that Complex staff will have to pioneer this effort. This may seem a daunting task, but placed in context, it is similar to the initiation of new work to document plant community composition and distribution. Of primary importance is documenting the current status of terrestrial soils, including profile descriptions, surface organic matter content, and nutrient properties. In addition, documenting water chemistry at periodic intervals (e.g., in relation to plant phenology), developing baseline references of sediment accrual, and monitoring plant community dynamics at critical times (e.g., germination, establishment) during the annual cycle represent primary needs for wetlands.

Finally, process-level information will be most valuable if placed in the context of a system because wetlands and grasslands are intricately connected components of a single landscape as evidenced by the transfer of energy and material. Thus, collecting information simultaneously on uplands and wetlands known to be linked will aid future interpretation. In addition, baseline information should be developed for the full range of current abiotic and biotic conditions (e.g., soils, slopes, existing vegetation) and detailed records should be maintained regarding management actions. This is critical to developing an understanding how and why the effectiveness of strategies differ among management units.

Literature Cited

American Ornithologists' Union. 2000. Forty-second supplement to the American Ornithologists' Union Check-list of North American Birds. Auk 117:847-858.

American Ornithologists' Union. 2002. Forty-third supplement to the American Ornithologists' Union Check-list of North American Birds. Auk 119:897-906.

American Ornithologists' Union. 2003. Forty-fourth supplement to the American Ornithologists' Union Check-list of North American Birds. Auk 120:923-931.

Baker, L. A. 1992. Introduction to nonpoint source pollution in the United States and prospects for wetland use. Ecological Engineering 1:1-26.

Beyersbergen, G. W., N. D. Niemuth, and M. R. Norton, [coordinators]. 2004. Northern Prairie and Parkland Waterbird Conservation Plan. Prairie Pothole Joint Venture, U.S. Fish and Wildlife Service, Denver, CO.

Bluemle, J. P. 2000. The face of North Dakota. 3rd ed. North Dakota Geological Survey, Education Series 26, Bismarck, ND.

Borthwick, S. M. 1988. Impacts of agricultural pesticides on aquatic invertebrates inhabiting prairie wetlands. M.S. thesis, Colorado State University, Fort Collins, CO.

Bragg, T. B., and A. A. Steuter. 1996. Mixed-grass prairies of the North American Great Plains, p. 53-66. In F. B. Samson and F. L. Knopf [eds.], Prairie conservation: preserving North America's most endangered ecosystem. Island Press, Covelo, CA.

Clayton, L. 1962. Glacial geology of Logan and McIntosh Counties, North Dakota. North Dakota Geological Survey Bulletin 37, Grand Forks, ND.

Coupland, R. T. 1950. Ecology of mixed prairie in Canada. Ecological Monographs 20:271-315.

Coupland, R. T. 1992. Approach and generalizations, p. 1-6. In R. T. Coupland [ed.], Ecosystems of the World 8A; natural grassland, introduction and Western Hemisphere. Elsevier, New York, NY.

Cowardin, L. M., D. S. Gilmer, and C. W. Shaifer. 1985. Mallard recruitment in the agricultural environment of North Dakota. Wildlife Monographs 92.

Dahl, T. E. 1990. Wetlands losses in the United States 1780's to 1980's. U.S. Department of the Interior, Fish and Wildlife Service, Washington, DC.

Dieter, C. D. 1991. Water turbidity in tilled and untilled prairie wetlands. Journal of Freshwater Ecology 6:185-189.

Euliss, N. H., Jr., and D. M. Mushet. 1999. Influence of agriculture on aquatic invertebrate communities of temporary wetlands in the prairie pothole region of North Dakota. Wetlands 19:578-583.

Euliss, N. H., Jr., J. W. LaBaugh, L. H. Fredrickson, D. M. Mushet, M. K. Laubhan, G. A. Swanson, T. C. Winter, D. O. Rosenberry, and R. D. Nelson. 2004. The wetland continuum: a conceptual framework for interpreting biological studies. Wetlands 24:448-458.

Euliss, N. H., Jr., D. A. Wrubleski, and D. M. Mushet. 1999. Invertebrates in wetlands of the prairie pothole region: species composition, ecology, and management, p. 471-513. In D. P. Batzer, R. B. Rader, and S. A. Wissinger [eds.], Invertebrates in freshwater wetlands of North America: ecology and management. John Wiley and Sons, New York, NY.

Fenneman, N. M. 1931. Physiography of western United States. McGraw-Hill, New York, NY.

Ferland, C. L., and S. M. Haig. 2002. 2001 international piping plover census. U.S. Geological Survey, Forest and Rangeland Ecosystem Science Center, Corvallis, OR.

Flint, R. F. 1955. Pleistocene geology of eastern South Dakota. U.S. Geological Survey Professional Paper 262, Washington, DC.

Flores, D. 1995. History, environment, and the future of the Great Plains, p. 3-9. In S. R. Johnson and A. Bouzaher [eds.], Conservation of Great Plains ecosystems: current science, future options. Kluwer Academic Publishers, Boston, MA.

Gambrell, R. P. 1994. Trace and toxic metals in wetlands: a review. Journal of Environmental Quality 23:883-892.

Gilliam, J. W. 1994. Riparian wetlands and water quality. Journal of Environmental Quality 23:896-900.

Gleason, R. A., and N. H. Euliss, Jr. 1998. Sedimentation of prairie wetlands. Great Plains Research 8:97-112.

Gleason, R. A., C. W. Holmes, D. E. Hubbard, and W. G. Duffy. 2003. Effects of sediment load on emergence of aquatic invertebrates and plants from wetland soil egg and seed banks. Wetlands 23:26-34.

Goldman, C. R., and A. J. Horne. 1983. Limnology. McGraw Hill, New York, NY.

Grant, T. A., E. M. Madden, R. K. Murphy, K. A. Smith, and M. P. Nenneman. 2004. Monitoring native prairie vegetation: the belt transect method. Ecological Restoration 22:106-112.

Grue, C. E., M. W. Tome, T. A. Messmer, D. B. Henry, G. A. Swanson, and L. R. DeWeese. 1989. Agricultural chemicals and prairie pothole wetlands: meeting the needs of the resource and the farmer – U. S. perspective. Transactions of the North American Wildlife and Natural Resources Conference 54:43-58.

Hanson, H. C., and W. Whitman. 1938. Characteristics of major grassland types in western North Dakota. Ecological Monographs 8:57-114.

Hartleb, C. F., J. D. Madsen, and C. W. Boylen. 1993. Environmental factors affecting seed germination in *Myriophyllum spicatum* L. Aquatic Botany 45:15-25.

Harrington, J. A., Jr., and J. R. Harman. 1995. Climate and vegetation in central North America: natural patterns and human alterations, p. 135-148. *In* S. R. Johnson and A. Bouzaher [eds.], Conservation of Great Plains ecosystems: current science, future options. Kluwer Academic Publishers, Boston, MA.

Huntzinger, T. L. 1995. Surface water: a critical resource of the Great Plains, p. 253-273. In S. R. Johnson and A. Bouzaher [eds.], Conservation of Great Plains ecosystems: current science, future options. Kluwer Academic Publishers, Boston, MA.

Jensen, M. E., P. Bourgeron, R. Everett, and I. Goodman. 1996. Ecosystem management: a landscape ecology perspective. Water Resources Bulletin 32:203-216.

Jensen, R. E. No Date. Climate of North Dakota. National Weather Service, North Dakota State University, Fargo, North Dakota. Jamestown, ND: Northern Prairie Wildlife Research Center Home Page. <http://www.npwrc.usgs.gov/resource/othrdata/climate/climate.htm> (17 January 2005).

Johnson, R. G., and S. A. Temple. 1986. Assessing habitat quality for birds nesting in fragmented tallgrass prairies, p. 245-249. *In* J. Verner, M. L. Morrison, and C. J. Ralph [eds.], Wildlife 2000: modeling habitat relationships of terrestrial vertebrates. University of Wisconsin Press, Madison, WI.

Jurik, T. W., S. Wang, and A.G. van der Valk. 1994. Effects of sediment load on seedling emergence from wetland seed banks. Wetlands 14:159-165.

Kantrud, H. A., and R. L. Kologiski. 1982. Ordination and classification of North Dakota grasslands. Proceedings of the North Dakota Academy of Science 36:35.

Kantrud, H. A., G. L. Krapu, and G. A. Swanson. 1989. Prairie basin wetlands of the Dakotas: a community profile. U.S. Fish and Wildlife Service, Biological Report 85, Washington, DC.

Klett, A. T., T. L. Shaffer, and D. H. Johnson. 1988. Duck nest success in the Prairie Pothole Region. Journal of Wildlife Management 52:431-440.

Knopf, F. L., and F. B. Samson. 1995. Conserving the biotic integrity of the Great Plains, p. 121-133. *In* S. R. Johnson and A. Bouzaher [eds.], Conservation of Great Plains ecosystems: current science, future options. Kluwer Academic Publishers, Boston, MA.

Konrad, P. M. 1996. Top 10 spring birding hotspots. Wildbird 10:28-33.

Kothmann, M. M. 1995. Rangeland ecosystems in the Great Plains: status and management, p. 199-209. *In* S. R. Johnson and A. Bouzaher [eds.], Conservation of Great Plains ecosystems: current science, future options. Kluwer Academic Publishers, Boston, MA.

Krull, J. N. 1970. Aquatic plant-macroinvertebrate associations and waterfowl. Journal of Wildlife Management 34:707-718.

Krupa, S. V., and A. H. Legge. 1995. Air quality, climate change, and their possible impacts on the terrestrial ecosystems of the North American Great Plains, p. 161-182. *In* S. R. Johnson and A. Bouzaher [eds.], Conservation of Great Plains ecosystems: current science, future options. Kluwer Academic Publishers, Boston, MA.

Kullberg, R. G. 1974. Distribution of aquatic macrophytes related to paper mill effluents in a southern Michigan stream. American Midland Naturalist 91:271-281.

Kume, J., and D. E. Hansen. 1965. Geology and ground water resources of Burleigh County, North Dakota: part I – geology. North Dakota Geological Survey Bulletin 42, Grand Forks, ND.

Kushlan, J. A., M. J. Steinkamp, K. C. Parsons, J. Capp, M. A. Cruz, M. Coulter, I. Davidson, L. Dickson, N. Edelson, R. Elliot, R. M. Erwin, S. Hatch S. Kress, R. Milko, S. Miller, K. Mills, R. Paul, R. Phillips, J. E. Saliva, B. Sydeman, J. Trapp, J. Wheeler, and K. Wohl. 2002. Waterbird Conservation for the Americas: The North American Waterbird Conservation Plan, version 1. Waterbird Conservation for the Americas, Washington, DC.

LaBaugh, J. W. 1989. Chemical characteristics of water in northern prairie wetlands, p. 56-90. *In* A. van der Valk [ed.], Northern prairie wetlands. Iowa State University, Ames, IA.

LaBaugh, J. W., T. C. Winter, V. A. Adomaitis, and G. A. Swanson. 1987. Hydrology and chemistry of selected prairie wetlands in the Cottonwood Lake area, Stutsman County, North Dakota, 1979-82. U.S. Geological Survey Professional Paper 1431, Washington, DC.

LaBaugh, J. W., and G. A. Swanson. 2004. Spatial and temporal variability in specific conductance and chemical characteristics of wetland water and in water column biota in the wetlands in the Cottonwood Lake area, p. 35-53. *In* T C. Winter [ed.], Hydrological, chemical, and biological characteristics of a prairie pothole wetland complex under highly variable climate conditions – the Cottonwood Lake area, east-central North Dakota. U.S Geological Survey Professional Paper 1675, Denver, CO.

Laubhan, M. K., and J. E. Roelle. 2001. Managing wetlands for waterbirds, p. 387-411. *In* R. B. Rader, D. P. Batzer, and S. Wissinger [eds.], Biomonitoring and management of North American Freshwater Wetlands. John Wiley and Sons, New York, NY.

Laubhan, M. K., S. L. King, and L. H. Fredrickson. 2005. Managing wetlands for wildlife, p. 797-838. In C. E. Braun [ed.], Techniques for wildlife investigations and management. 6th ed. Allen Press, Lawrence, KS.

Lemke, R. W. 1960. Geology of the Souris River area, North Dakota. U.S. Geological Survey Professional Paper 325, Washington, DC.

Lemke, R. W., and R. B. Colton. 1958. Summary of the Pleistocene geology of North Dakota. North Dakota Geological Survey Miscellaneous Series 10:41-57, Grand Forks, ND.

Lissey, A. 1971. Depression-focused transient groundwater flow patterns in Manitoba. Geological Association of Canada Special Paper 9:333-341, Montreal, QUE.

Lock, L. N., and M. Friend. 1989. Avian botulism: geographic expansion of a historic disease. U.S. Fish and Wildlife Service, Waterfowl Management Handbook, Fish and Wildlife Leaflet 13.2.4, Washington, DC.

Longcore, J. R., R. K. Ross, and K. L. Fisher. 1987. Wildlife resources at risk through acidification of wetlands. Transactions of the North American Wildlife and Natural Resources Conference 52:608-618.

Mayfield, H. F. 1961. Nesting success calculated from exposure. Wilson Bulletin 73:255-261.

McEnroe, M. 1986. Avian botulism in North Dakota. North Dakota Outdoors 48:6.

Metcalf, F. P. 1931. Wild-duck foods of North Dakota lakes. U.S. Department of Agriculture, Technical Bulletin No. 221, Washington, DC.

Murkin, H. R., and B. D. J. Batt. 1987. The interactions of vertebrates and invertebrates in peatlands and marshes. Memoirs of the Entomological Society of Canada 140:15-30.

Newcombe, C. P., and D. D. MacDonald. 1991. Effects of suspended sediments on aquatic ecosystems. North American Journal of Fisheries Management 11:72-82.

Olson, M. M., and D. Welsh. 1991. An investigation into the water quality of Long Lake National Wildlife Refuge, Burleigh and Kidder Counties, North Dakota. U.S. Fish and Wildlife Service, Environmental Contaminants Program, Bismarck, ND. <http://ecos.fws.gov/dec_reports/73/report.html> (17 January 2005)

Peterson, G. A., and C. V. Cole. 1995. Productivity of Great Plains soils: past, present, and future, p. 325-342. *In* S. R. Johnson and A. Bouzaher [eds.], Conservation of Great Plains ecosystems: current science, future options. Kluwer Academic Publishers, Boston, MA.

Rainwater, F. H., and L.L. Thatcher. 1960. Methods for collection and analysis of water samples. U.S. Geological Survey Water Supply Paper 1454, Washington, DC.

Randich, P. G., and J. L. Hatchett. 1966. Geology and ground water resources of Burleigh County, North Dakota: Part III – ground water resources. North Dakota Geological Survey Bulletin 42, Grand Forks, ND.

Randich, P. G., L. R. Petri, and D. G. Adolphson. 1962. Geology and ground water resources of Kidder County, North Dakota: Part II – ground water basic data. North Dakota Geological Survey Bulletin 36, Grand Forks, ND.

Rau, J. L., W. E. Bakken, J. Chmelik, and B. J. Williams. 1962. Geology and ground water resources of Kidder County, North Dakota; Part I geology. North Dakota Geological Survey Bulletin 36, Grand Forks, ND.

Reynolds, R. E., D. R. Cohan, and C. R. Loesch. 1997. Wetlands of North and South Dakota. Jamestown, North Dakota: Northern Prairie Wildlife Research Center Home Page. <http://www.npwrc.usgs.gov/resource/wetlands/wetstats/wetstats.htm> (17 January 2005).

Rich, T. D., C. J. Beardmore, H. Berlanga, P. J. Blancher, M. S. W. Bradstreet, G. S. Butcher, D. W. Demarest, E. H. Dunn, W. C. Hunter, E. E. Iñigo-Elias, J. A. Kennedy, A. M. Martell, A. O. Panjabi, D. N. Pashley, K. V. Rosenberg, C. M. Rustay, J. S. Wendt, T. C. Will. 2004. Partners in Flight North American Landbird Conservation Plan, Cornell Laboratory of Ornithology, Ithaca, NY.

Robel, R. J. 1961. Water depth and turbidity in relation to growth of sago pondweed. Journal of Wildlife Management 25:436-438.

Rocke, T. E., N. H. Euliss, and M. D. Samuel. 1999. Environmental characteristics associated with the occurrence of avian botulism in wetlands of a northern California refuge. Journal of Wildlife Management 63:358-368.

Rosenberg, N. J. 1987. Climate of the Great Plains region of the United States. Great Plains Quarterly 7:22-32.

Rybicki, N. B., and V. Carter. 1986. Effect of sediment depth and sediment type on the survival of *Vallisneria americana* Michx grown form tubers. Aquatic Botany 24:233-240.

Salisbury, F. B., and C. W. Ross. 1978. Mineral nutrition, p. 79-92. In J. C. Carey and G. H. Bookworks [eds.], Plant physiology. 2nd ed. Wadsworth Publishing, Belmont, CA.

Samson, F. B. 1980. Island biogeography and the conservation of prairie birds. North American Prairie Conference 7:293-305.

Samson, F. B., F. L. Knopf, and W. R. Ostlie. 1998. Grasslands, p. 437-472. *In* M. J. Mac, P. A. Opler, C. E. Puckett Haecker, and P. D. Doran [eds.], Status and Trends of the Nation's Biological Resources. Volume 2. Jamestown, ND: Northern Prairie Wildlife Research Center Home Page. <http://www.npwrc.usgs.gov/resource/wetlands/wetstats/wetstats.htm> (17 January 2005).

Sarvis, J. T. 1920. Composition and density of the native vegetation in the vicinity of the Northern Great Plains Field Station. Journal of Agricultural Research 19:63-72.

Saucier. R. T. 1994. Geomorphology and quaternary geological history of the Lower Mississippi Valley. Volumes 1 and 2. U.S. Department of the Army, U.S. Army Corps of Engineers Waterways Experiment Station, Vicksburg, MI.

Seelig, B., and A. R. Gulsvig. 1988. Soil survey of Kidder County, North Dakota. U.S. Government Printing Office, Washington, DC.

Shjeflo, J. B. 1968. Evapotranspiration and the water budget of prairie potholes in North Dakota. U.S. Geological Survey Professional Paper 585-B, Washington, DC.

Simpson, E. H. 1949. Measurement of diversity. Nature 163:688.

Skagen, S. K., and G. Thompson. 2003. Northern Plains/Prairie Potholes Regional Shorebird Conservation Plan. U. S. Shorebird Conservation Plan. <http://shorebirdplan.fws.gov/RegionalShorebird/downloads/NORPLPP2.doc> (17 January 2005).

Sopuck, R. D. 1995. Sustaining the Great Plains ecosystem: integrating people, economics, and the landscape, p. 83-95. *In* S. R. Johnson and A. Bouzaher [eds.], Conservation of Great Plains ecosystems: current science, future options. Kluwer Academic Publishers, Boston, MA.

Stewart, R. E., and H. A. Kantrud. 1971. Classification of natural ponds and lakes in the glaciated prairie region. Bureau of Sport Fisheries and Wildlife Resource Publication 92, Washington, DC.

Stewart, R. E., and H. A. Kantrud. 1972. Vegetation of prairie potholes, North Dakota, in relation to quality of water and other environmental factors. U.S. Geological Survey Professional Paper 585-D, Washington, DC.

Stout, H. R., W. F. Freymiller, F. J. Glatt, R. D. Heil, M. C. McVay, J. H. Thiele, and P. K. Weiser. 1974. Soil survey of Burleigh County, North Dakota. U.S. Government Printing Office, Washington, DC.

Swanson, G. A., T. C. Winter, V. A. Adomaitis, and J. W. LaBaugh. 1988. Chemical characteristics of prairie lakes in south-central North Dakota – their potential for influencing use by fish and wildlife. U.S. Fish and Wildlife Service, Technical Report 18, Washington, DC.

Taylor, J. R., M. A. Cardamone, and W. J. Mitsch. 1990. Bottomland hardwood forests: their functions and values, p. 13-86. *In* L. C. Lee, J. G. Gosselink, and T. A. Muir [eds.], Ecological processes and cumulative impacts illustrated by bottomland hardwood wetland ecosystems. Lewis Publishers, Chelsea, MI.

Ulrich, R. A., and F. K. Pfeifer. 1976. Limnological survey of the Souris River and its major tributaries in North Dakota: October 1975. U.S. Fish and Wildlife Service, Division of Fishery Services, Bismarck Area Office, Bismarck, ND.

U.S. Fish and Wildlife Service. 1988. Botulism briefing handout. Unpublished Report, Long Lake National Wildlife Refuge, Moffit, ND.

U.S. Fish and Wildlife Service. 1996. MAAPE duck management plan for the Long Lake Wetland Management District. Unpublished Report, Long Lake National Wildlife Refuge, Moffit, ND.

U.S. Fish and Wildlife Service. 2002. Birds of conservation concern 2002. Division of Migratory Bird Management, Arlington, VA. <http://migratorybirds.fws.gov/reports/bcc2002.pdf> (17 January 2005).

U.S. Prairie Pothole Joint Venture. 1995. U. S. Prairie Pothole Joint Venture Implementation Plan (update). Northern Prairie Wildlife Research Center Home Page, Jamestown, ND. <http://www.npwrc.usgs.gov/resource/2001/impplan/impplan.htm> (17 January 2005).

Wang, S., T. W. Jurik, and A. G. van der Valk. 1994. Effects of sediment load on various stages in the life and death of cattail (*Typha x Glauca*). Wetlands 14:166-173.

Whitman, W. C. 1941. The native grassland, p. 5-7. *In* Grass. North Dakota Agricultural Experiment Station Research Bulletin 300, Fargo, ND.

Wimmer, M. A., K. H. Mühling, A. Läuchli, P. H. Brown, and H. E. Goldbach. 2003. The interaction between salinity and boron toxicity affects the subcellular distribution of ions and proteins in wheat leaves. Plant, Cell, and Environment 26:1267-1274.

Winter, T. C. 1977. Classification of the hydrologic settings of lakes in the north central United States. Water Resources Research 13:753-767.

Winter, T. C. 2003. Hydrological, chemical, and biological characteristics of a Prairie Pothole wetland complex under highly variable climate conditions – the Cottonwood Lake area, east-central North Dakota. U.S. Geological Survey Professional Paper 1675, Denver, CO.

Winter, T. C., R. D. Benson, R. A. Engberg, G. J. Wiche, D. G. Emerson, O. A. Crosby, and J. E. Miller. 1984. Synopsis of ground-water and surface-water resources of North Dakota. U.S. Geological Survey Open-File Report 84-732, Reston, VA.

Wobeser, G. 1997. Avian botulism – another perspective. Journal of Wildlife Disease 33:181-186.

Wobeser, G., and T. Bollinger. 2002. Type C botulism – management dilemma. Transactions of the North American Wildlife and Natural Resources Conference 67:40-50.

Wollheim, W. M., and J. R. Lovvorn. 1996. Effects of macrophyte growth forms on invertebrate communities in saline lakes of the Wyoming High Plains. Hydrobiologia 323:83-96.

Table 1. General physical properties of soil associations occurring on Long Lake, Slade, and Florence Lake National Wildlife Refuges (Stout et al. 1974, Seelig and Gulsvig 1988).

National Wildlife Refuge	Soil Association	Soil Types	Material	Soil Depth	Soil Texture	Available Water Capacity
Long Lake	Roseglen-Tansem-Savage	Loam, silt loam, silty clay loam	Glacial lake plain, terrace	Deep	Medium	Moderate to high
	Parshall-Lihen-Flaxton	Fine sandy loam, loamy fine sand	Glacial outwash	Deep	Coarse to moderately coarse	Moderate
	Williams-Max-Zahl	Loam	Glacial till	Deep	Medium	High
	Williams-Max	Loam, clay loam	Glacial	Deep	Medium	High
	Telfer-Lihen-Seroco	Loamy sand, loamy fine sand	Wind deposited sand	Deep	Coarse, sand-mantled	Very low to moderate
	Harriet-Minnewaukan-Stirum	Sandy loam, loamy fine sand, fine sand	Glacial outwash, lacustrine sediment	Deep	Medium	Very low
	Williams-Bowbells	Loam, clay loam	Glacial till	Deep	Medium	Very low
	Arvilla	Sandy loam, loamy sand,	Glacial outwash	Deep	Medium	Very low
Florence Lake	Lehr-Wabek-Manning	Loam, gravelly loam, sandy loam	Glacial outwash	Moderately deep to shallow	Medium to moderately coarse	Very low to low
Slade	Arvilla	Sandy loam, loamy sand	Glacial outwash	Deep	Medium	Very low

Table 2. Properties of common soil series underlying wetland basins on Long Lake, Slade, and Florence Lake National Wildlife Refuges (Stout et al. 1974).

Soil Series	Soil Association	Material	Permeability	Available Water Capacity	Organic Matter	Fertility
Arnegard	Williams-Max-Zahl Williams-Max Roseglen-Tansem-Savage	Local alluvium	Moderate	High	High	High
Arveson	Harriet-Minnewauken-Stirum	Glacial deposits	Moderately rapid	Low	High	Medium
Belfield	Roseglen-Tansem-Savage	Soft shale or silstone	Moderately slow	High	Medium	Medium
Daglum	Roseglen-Tansem-Savage	Alluvium from shale or siltstone	Slow	Moderate	Medium	Medium
Noonan	Williams-Bowbells	Loamy glacial till	Slow	Moderate	Medium	Medium
Parnell	Williams-Max Zahl Williams-Max Williams-Bowbells	Local alluvium	Slow	High	High	High
Regan	Lakes	Alluvium	Moderate	Moderate	High	Medium
Rhoades	Roseglen-Tansem-Savage	Alluvium from shale or shale	Very slow	Low	Medium	Low
Roseglen	Lakes	Lacustrine sediments and glacial outwash	Moderate	High	High	High
Savage	Lakes	Deep clay sediments	Slow	High	Medium	Medium
Straw	Roseglen-Tansem-Savage	Alluvium	Moderate	High	High	High
Tansem	Lakes	Lacustrine sediments and glacial outwash	Moderate	High	Medium	Medium
Tonka	Williams-Max-Zahl	Local alluvium	Slow	High	High	Medium

Table 3. Concentrations of select constituents in water from glacial drift in the vicinity of Long Lake, Harker Lake, and Florence Lake in Burleigh and Kidder counties, North Dakota (Randich et al. 1962, Randich and Hatchett 1966). Specific conductance measured in mmhos per cm, dissolved solids = residue on evaporation at 180 C in ppm, Fe = iron, B = boron, Mg = magnesium, Na = sodium, K = potassium, HCO_3 = bicarbonate, SO_4 = sulfate).

National Wildlife Refuge (township/range/section)	Material	pH	Specific conductance	Dissolved solids	Concentration (ppm)						
					Fe	B	Mg	Na	K	HCO_3	SO_4
Long Lake (137N/74W/11)	Glacial outwash in till	7.3	1030	661	1.10	0.53	22.0	176	79	513	131.0
Long Lake (137N/75W/22)	Glacial drift	7.7	734	458	0.26	0.25	18.0	33	7.0	329	94.0
Long Lake (137N/76W/5)	Foxhills sandstone	8.4	2496	1,510	0.78	0.00	1.2	610	1.8	1,153	2.7
Long Lake (137N/76W/26)	Glacial drift	8.1	1223	829	1.34	0.00	8.5	246	13.0	641	112.0
Long Lake (138N/73W/17)	Glacial outwash	7.3	1160	751	0.15	0.61	14.0	200	10	573	110.0
Slade (138N/72W/2)	Glacial outwash	7.2	918	586	0.51	0.39	27.0	111	11	436	130.0
Florence (144N/76W/18)	Glacial drift	7.9	1052	639	0.17	0.00	...	33	0.0	380	165.0

Table 4. Distribution of wetland types in Burleigh and Kidder counties, North Dakota (Reynolds et al. 1997).

Wetland type	Burleigh County		Kidder County	
	Area (ha)	Basins per km^2	Area (ha)	Basins per km^2
Temporary	3370	1.93	3344	2.47
Seasonal	9714	6.16	10,109	6.66
Semipermanent	11,952	0.53	15,053	1.02
Lake	11,024	0.01	24,313	0.05
River	2281	0.05	12	0.00
Total	38,342	8.68	52,831	10.15

Table 5. Area (ha) of cover classes on Long Lake National Wildlife Refuge in 2003.

Cover class	Hectares	# Polygons
Wetlands		
Temporary	116.14	38
Seasonal	25.55	90
Semipermanent	186.52	76
Lake	6557.65	9
Riverine	5.80	4
Non-NWI wetland	204.60	265
Subtotal wetlands	7096.55	482
Noxious weeds		
Canada thistle > 50%	29.52	391
Absinth wormwood > 50%	25.94	284
Leafy spurge > 50%	0.32	35
Subtotal noxious weeds	55.78	710
Grasses		
Non-native grasses/forbs > 95%	1294.71	273
Non-native/native mix, non-natives > 50%	125.10	172
Exotic C3 grasses and legumes (DNC)	71.48	16
Crested wheatgrass monotype	5.61	18
Smooth brome monotype	0.70	5
Other undesirable plants > 50%	21.77	26
Native/non-native mix, natives > 50%	11.47	42
Subtotal grasses	1530.85	552
Low shrubs		
Western snowberry	153.27	333
Subtotal low shrubs	153.27	333
Tall shrubs		
Russian olive	2.73	122
Chokecherry, juneberry, hawthorn association	1.91	97
Willow	0.84	17
Buffaloberry	0.53	13
Rocky Mountain juniper	0.28	1
Caragana	0.21	1
Unknown and/or dead	1.47	9
Subtotal tall shrubs	7.98	260
Trees		
Green ash, box elder, elm association	1.57	33
Cottonwood	1.07	34
Tree/tall shrub mix	13.21	14
Mixed forest, tree/tall shrub, dead or unknown	2.63	65
Subtotal trees	18.48	146
Croplands		
Small grain	132.84	10
Row	8.72	1
Subtotal croplands	141.55	11
Other		
Gravel road/trail	10.82	11
Headquarters	2.17	1
Wildfire area	1.02	1
Old headquarters	0.90	1
Gravel pit	0.36	1
Picnic area	0.17	1
Mowed area	0.11	2
Subtotal other	15.55	18
Total uplands	1923.46	2030
Total Long Lake National Wildlife Refuge area	9020.01	2512

Table 6. Frequency of occurrence of terrestrial plant associations based on 25-m belt transects in Unit G-6 (*n* = 18 transects) and virgin sod units (Units G-4A, G-4B, G-4C, G-9A, and G-9B; *n* = 74 transects) on Long Lake in 2004 and Florence Lake (*n* = 50 transects) National Wildlife Refuges in 2002.

Invasion extent	Plant association	Frequency of occurrence (%)		
		Long Lake G-6	Long Lake Virgin sod	Florence Lake
Low	Dry warm-season grasses		0.08	0.04
	Dry cool-season grasses	1.56	4.09	0.68
	Forbs co-dominant with native grass (25 - 75% each)	12.11	7.09	2.84
	Dwarf shrub with remainder mostly native grass		0.16	
	Native low shrub with remainder mostly native grass		1.71	0.40
	Forbs dominant (> 75%)	20.22	1.46	0.04
	Native low shrub dominant		0.16	
	Native tall shrub dominant		0.33	
	Total	33.89	15.08	4.00
Moderate	Native grass/smooth brome mixed (brome 25 - 50%)		1.14	0.44
	Native grass/Kentucky bluegrass (bluegrass 25 - 50%)		0.16	
	Dwarf shrub with remainder mostly non-native grass		0.46	0.60
	Natives/leafy spurge (25 - 75% each)		0.14	
	Native grass/sweet clover or alfalfa (25 - 75% each)	0.55	0.71	0.12
	Native grass/crested wheatgrass (25 - 75% each)	1.78	2.57	2.36
	Native grass/other exotic wheatgrass (25 - 75% each)			0.04
	Forbs/non-native grass (25 - 75% each)	4.11	13.15	31.0
	Native low shrub with remainder mostly non-native		4.65	4.84
	Total	6.44	22.98	39.40
High	Smooth brome > 95%	3.00	2.79	33.32
	Kentucky bluegrass > 95%		2.27	
	Smooth brome/Kentucky bluegrass (25 - 75% each)	30.78	38.03	
	Smooth brome/natives (brome 50 - 95%)	0.67	0.65	2.80
	Kentucky bluegrass/natives (bluegrass 50 - 95%)	0.78	2.55	
	Crested wheatgrass > 95%	8.44	7.01	6.96
	Crested wheatgrass/non-natives (25 - 75% each)	2.00	7.14	0.68
	Other exotic wheatgrass/non-natives (25 - 75% each)			1.12
	Leafy spurge > 95%		0.11	
	Leafy spurge/non-natives (25 - 75% each)		0.05	
	Sweet clover or alfalfa > 95%	11.89	0.08	
	Residual sweet clover dominant		0.02	
	Non-native grass/sweet clover or alfalfa (25 - 75% each)	2.11	1.24	11.76
	Non-native grass/Canada thistle (25 - 75% each)			0.16
	Absinth wormwood			0.48
	Total	59.67	61.94	57.28

Table 7. Waterfowl breeding population estimates and recruitment rates based on four square mile surveys (area = 12,108 km²) conducted on Long Lake National Wildlife Refuge Complex (including the Wetland Management District) between 1987 and 2004. Estimates based on pair data and recruitment rates of 13[a] and 5[b] primary waterfowl species breeding in the Prairie Pothole Region, respectively.

Year	Wet Area (km2)	Number Wet Ponds	Number pairs	Recruitment rate
1987	814.0	60,995	259,214	0.73
1988	525.5	22,302	115,709	0.47
1989	434.1	30,698	60,369	0.51
1990	196.3	11,400	8865	0.41
1991	232.1	8486	14,039	0.40
1992	280.2	26,236	55,205	0.46
1993	516.4	42,778	136,872	0.56
1994	802.9	76,675	285,481	0.80
1995	897.4	60,033	322,076	0.70
1996	950.3	63,317	358,755	0.72
1997	1263.4	78,460	544,017	0.82
1998	850.6	33,896	317,566	0.54
1999	1020.5	73,551	348,775	0.79
2000	1037.0	54,644	462,614	0.66
2001	1050.8	58,819	218,093	0.66
2002	816.4	35,986	194,093	0.53
2003	757.6	32,816	122,709	0.53
2004	636.4	26,805	131,847	0.50

[a] Includes Mallard, Gadwall, Blue-winged Teal, Northern Shoveler, Northern Pintail, American Wigeon, Green-winged Teal, Wood Duck, Redhead, Canvasback, Lesser Scaup, Ring-necked Duck, and Ruddy Duck.

[b] Includes Mallard, Gadwall, Blue-winged Teal, Northern Shoveler, and Northern Pintail.

Table 8. Nest success (Mayfield 1961) of upland-nesting waterfowl on seven management units of Long Lake National Wildlife Refuge during 2002 and six Waterfowl Production Areas in the Long Lake Wetland Management District during 2001.

	Number of nests		Mayfield nest success (%)	
	Total	Successful	Mean	95% Confidence intervals
National Wildlife Refuge				
Unit G-19E	3	0	0.4	0.0 - 100.0
Unit G-19W	9	3	17.8	4.2 - 70.8
Unit A-15	11	2	1.7	0.1 - 23.1
Unit G-17	15	3	3.0	0.4 - 21.6
Unit G-20	6	1	0.7	0.0 - 45.6
Unit G-4A	12	2	3.0	0.3 - 25.8
Unit G-5	23	3	1.8	0.3 - 10.5
Total	79	14	3.0	1.2 - 7.1
Waterfowl Production Area				
Basaraba	9	3	4.2	0.3 - 50.9
Bernhardt	16	10	38.8	17.7 - 83.3
Goldsmith	4	2	21.8	2.3 - 100.0
North Crimmins	52	34	35.4	21.6 - 57.5
Rath/Wonnenburg	13	4	7.5	1.3 - 40.4
Wahl	16	9	32.0	13.4 - 74.9
Total	110	62	26.8	18.3 - 39.1

Table 9. Number of colonial waterbird breeding pairs, number of colonies, and distribution of breeding pairs among wetland probability classes on Long Lake National Wildlife Refuge during 2003.

Species	Breeding pairs	Number of colonies	Distribution of breeding pairs among wetland probability classes[a]		
			High	Moderate	Low
Black-crowned Night-Heron	68	2	68	0	0
Black Tern	94	15	84	10	0
California Gull	310	4	310	0	0
Cattle Egret	104	1	104	0	0
Common Tern	295	6	295	0	0
Double-crested Cormorant	474	5	474	0	0
Eared Grebe	214	17	196	18	0
Franklin's Gull	66	2	66	0	0
Forster's Tern	162	4	162	0	0
Red-necked Grebe	4	3	4	0	0
Snowy Egret	3	1	3	0	0
Western Grebe/Clark's Grebe	120	6	120	0	0
White-faced Ibis	15	2	15	0	0

[a] Wetland probability class determined based on habitat conditions, including wetland cover type, hydrologic regime, basin size, and special features (e.g., islands, dead trees in wetland).

Table 10. Relative abundance, estimated breeding pairs/100 ha, and frequency of occurrence of 15 grassland/wetland edge nesting passerines on Long Lake National Wildlife Refuge, 2001-2004.

Species	Relative abundance (± SE)				Estimated pairs/100 ha				Occurrence (%)			
	2001	2002	2003	2004	2001	2002	2003	2004	2001	2002	2003	2004
Baird's Sparrow	0.02 (0.02)	0.00	0.00	0.02 (0.02)	0.6	0.0	0.0	0.6	2	0	0	2
Bobolink	1.72 (0.18)	1.34 (0.18)	1.26 (0.15)	1.68 (0.26)	54.8	42.7	40.1	53.5	80	66	74	66
Chestnut-collared Longspur	0.02 (0.02)	0.04 (0.03)	0.02 (0.02)	0.06 (0.03)	0.6	1.3	0.6	1.9	2	4	2	6
Clay-colored Sparrow	0.94 (0.17)	0.92 (0.17)	0.86 (0.15)	1.00 (0.19)	29.9	29.3	27.4	31.9	50	48	54	56
Common Yellowthroat	0.34 (0.09)	0.32 (0.09)	0.22 (0.07)	0.62 (0.18)	10.8	10.2	7.0	19.7	26	24	20	44
Grasshopper Sparrow	0.36 (0.11)	0.68 (0.13)	0.88 (0.14)	1.66 (0.22)	11.5	21.7	28.0	52.9	22	40	58	66
Lark Bunting	0.00	0.00	0.00	0.02 (0.20)	0.0	0.0	0.0	0.6	0	0	0	2
Le Conte's Sparrow	0.04 (0.03)	0.12 (0.03)	0.02 (0.02)	0.02 (0.02)	1.3	3.8	0.6	0.6	4	10	2	2
Nelson's Sharp-tailed Sparrow	0.04 (0.03)	0.00	0.00	0.04 (0.03)	1.30	0.0	0.0	1.3	4	0	0	4
Red-winged Blackbird	1.06 (0.22)	1.14 (0.25)	0.78 (0.14)	1.06 (0.22)	33.8	36.3	24.8	33.8	44	46	50	46
Savannah Sparrow	0.54 (0.13)	0.34 (0.08)	0.38 (0.10)	0.50 (0.13)	17.2	10.8	12.1	15.9	34	28	26	28
Sedge Wren	1.18 (0.20)	0.56 (0.16)	0.26 (0.11)	0.30 (0.10)	37.6	17.8	8.3	9.6	56	26	12	24
Sprague's Pipit	0.02 (0.02)	0.00	0.00	0.02 (0.02)	0.6	0.0	0.0	0.6	2	0	0	2
Vesper Sparrow	0.00	0.00	0.04 (0.03)	0.00	0.0	0.0	1.3	0.0	0	0	4	0
Western Meadowlark	0.30 (0.08)	0.06 (0.03)	0.44 (0.08)	0.57 (0.10)	9.6	1.9	14.0	18.2	24	6	40	46

Table 11. Internal tissue concentrations of essential elements that are considered adequate for most higher plants (Salisbury and Ross 1978).

Element	Dry tissue concentration (mg/L)
Micronutrients	
Molybdenum	0.1
Copper	6
Zinc	20
Manganese	50
Boron	20
Iron	100
Chlorine	100
Macronutrients	
Sulfur	1,000
Phosphorus	2,000
Magnesium	2,000
Calcium	5,000
Potassium	10,000
Nitrogen	15,000
Oxygen	450,000
Carbon	60,000

Figure 1. Location of Long Lake, Slade, and Florence Lake National Wildlife Refuges, and associated waterfowl production areas, in Burleigh, Emmons, and Kidder counties, North Dakota.

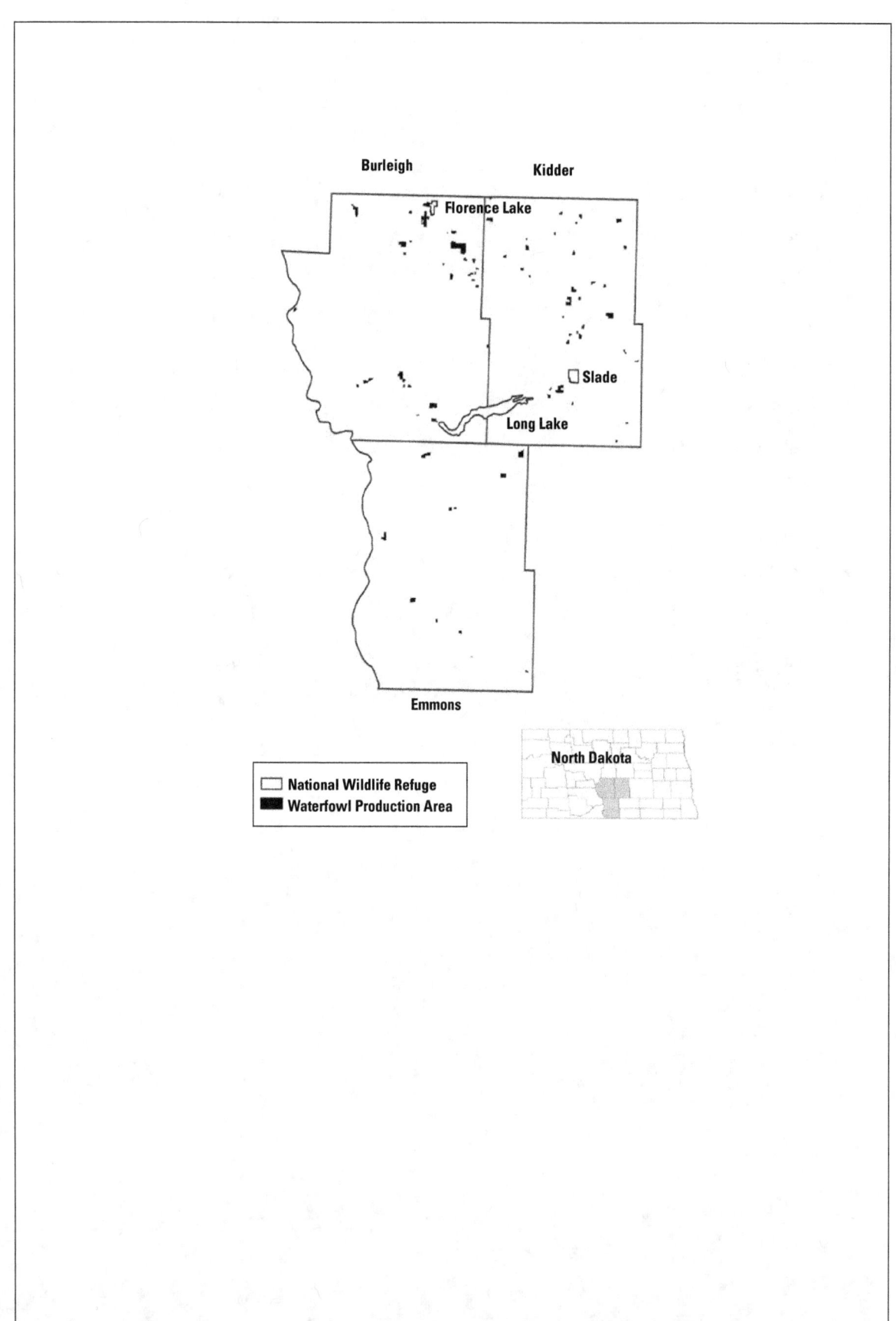

Figure 2. Estimated annual number of avian deaths (waterfowl and other birds) due to botulism on Long Lake National Wildlife Refuge, 1937-2004.

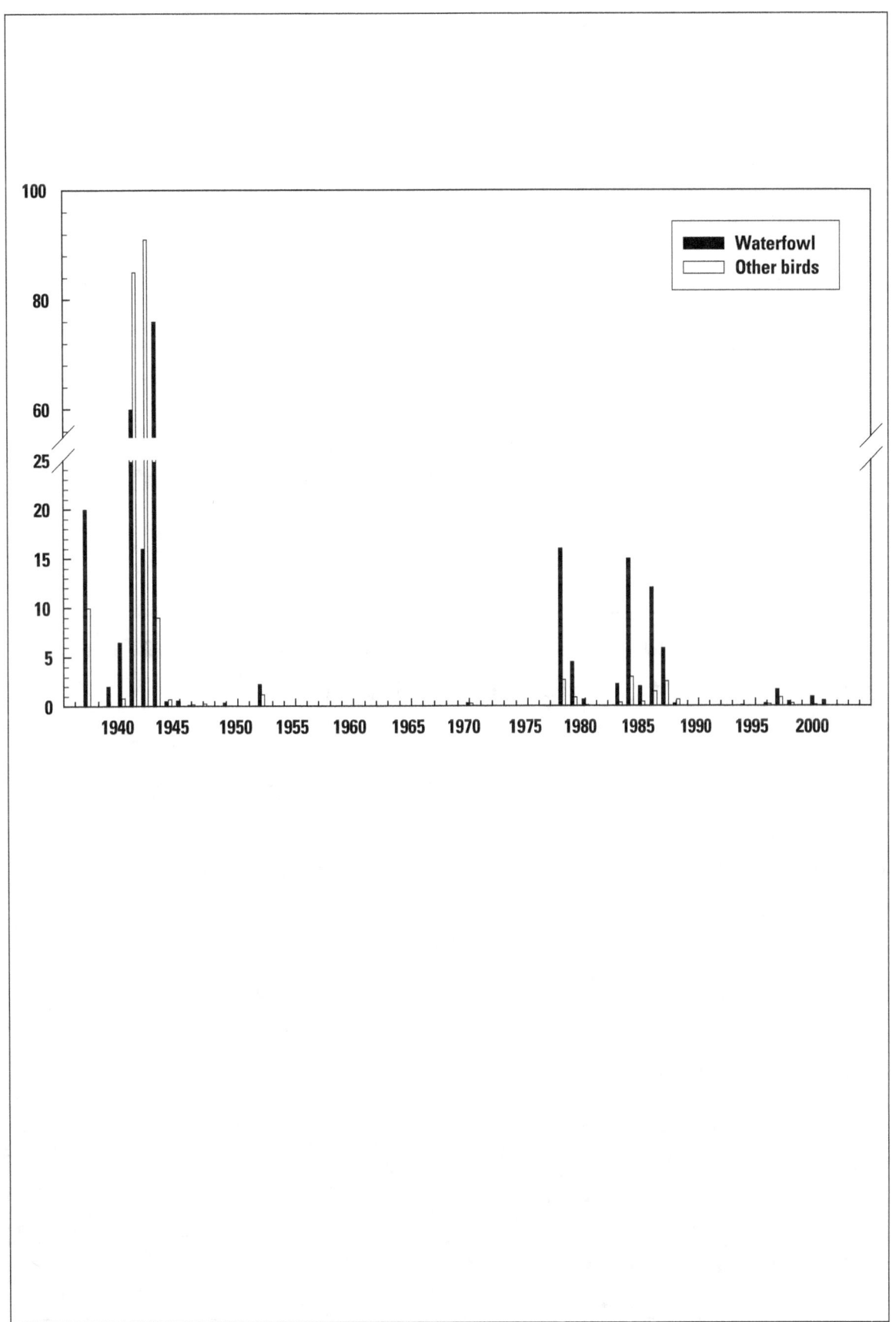

Figure 3. Relationship between specific conductance (µS per cm) and dissolved matter (mg per L).

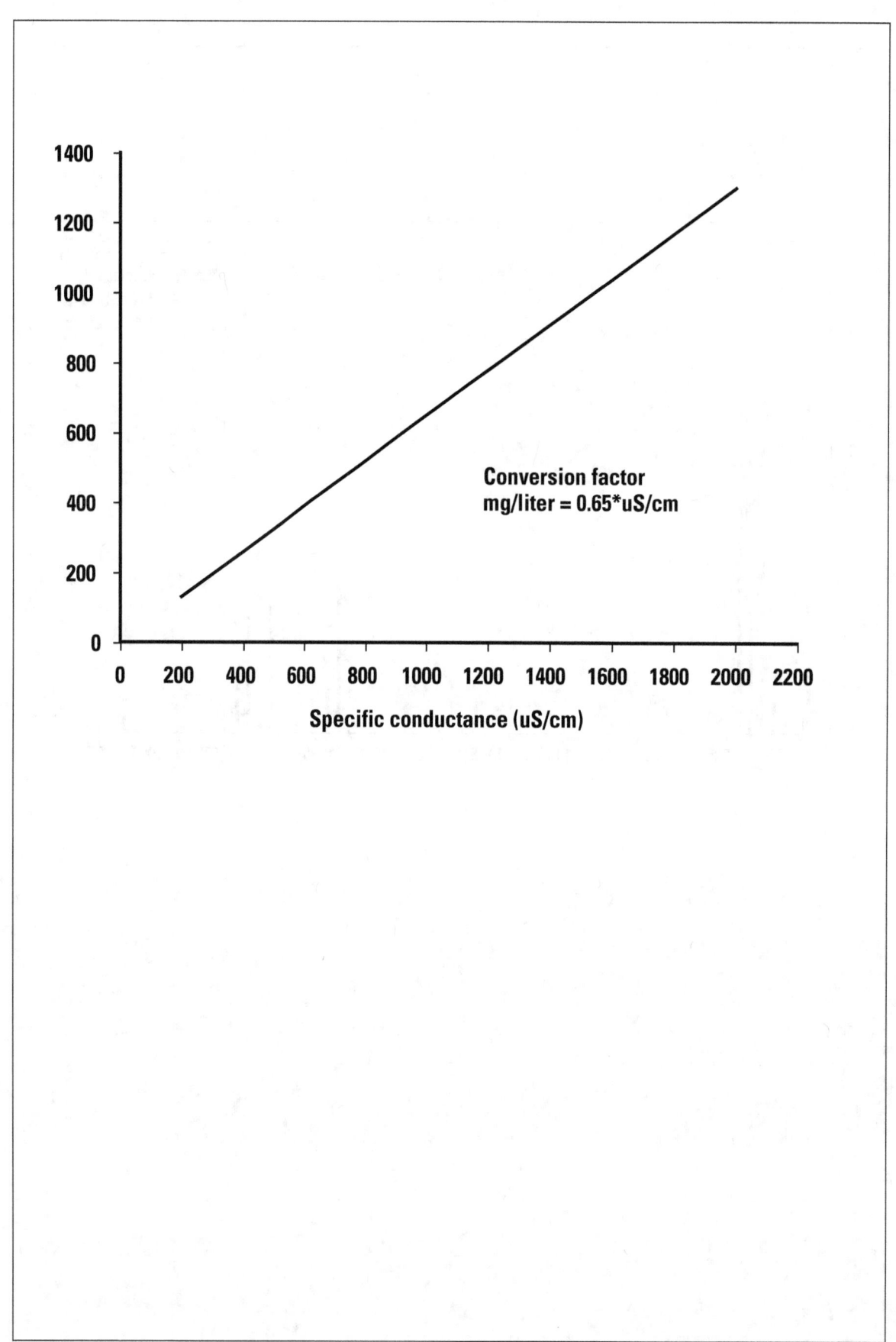

Figure 4. Estimated potential accumulation (tons) of evaporates per 30.5 cm of water that evaporates from Units 1, 2, and 3 on Long Lake National Wildlife Refuge.

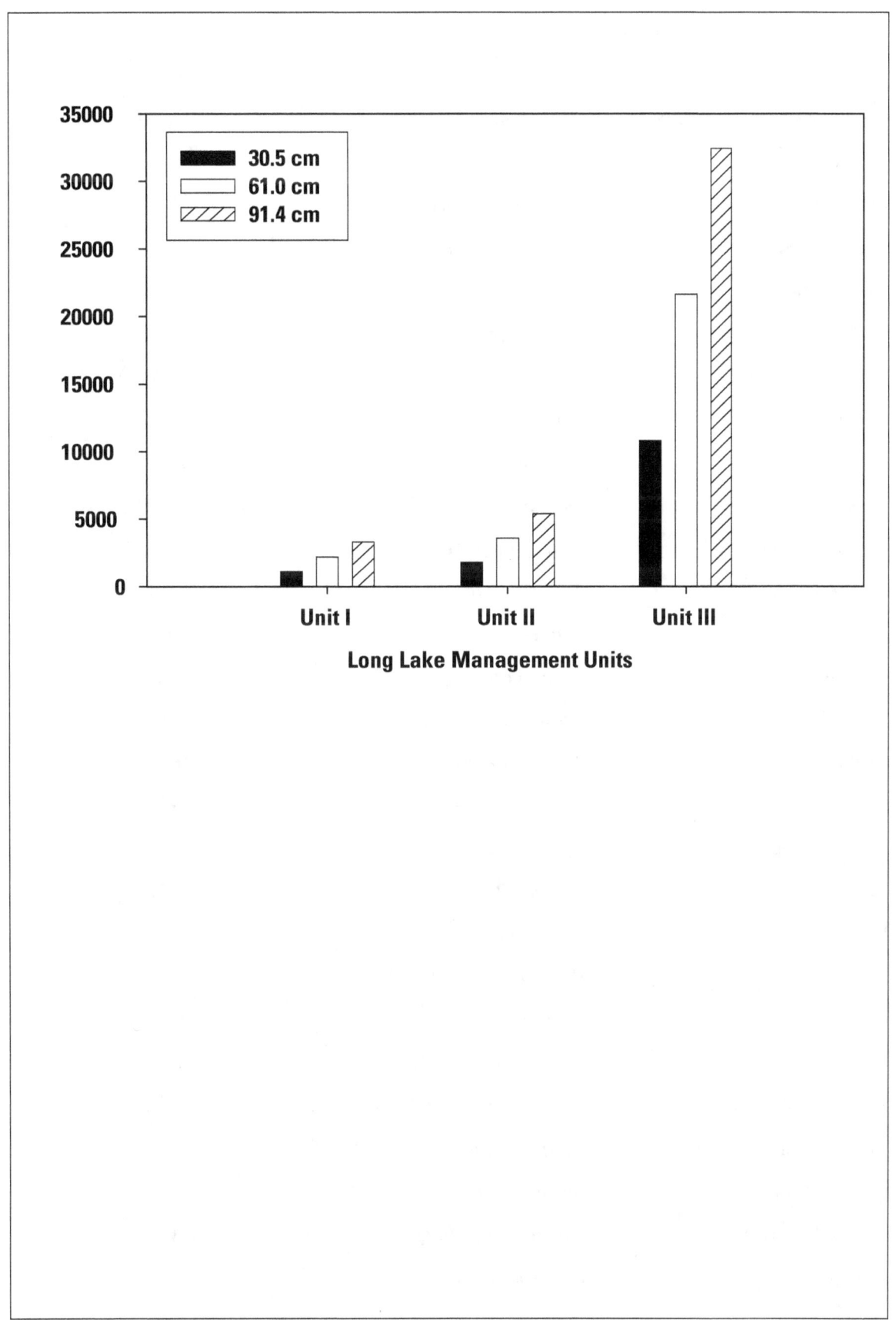

Appendix A. Scientific and common names of animals and plants mentioned in text. Naming convention of birds follow the American Ornithologists' Union Committee on Classification and Nomenclature (1998, 2000, 2002, 2003). Naming conventions of mammals and plants follow the Integrated Taxonomic Information System[a]. Bird names in bold indicate nesting species at Long Lake NWR and codes are provided for species that appear in Appendix C.

Common name	Scientific name	Species code
Birds		
Greater White-fronted Goose	*Anser albifrons*	GWFG
Snow Goose	*Chen caerulescens*	
Canada Goose	***Branta canadensis***	
Trumpeter Swan	*Cygnus buccinator*	
Tundra Swan	*Cygnus columbianus*	TUSW
Gadwall	***Anas strepera***	GADW
American Wigeon	*Anas americana*	AMWI
American Black Duck	*Anas rubripes*	
Mallard	***Anas platyrhynchos***	MALL
Blue-winged Teal	***Anas discors***	BWTE, TEAL
Cinnamon Teal	***Anas cyanoptera***	CITE, TEAL
Northern Shoveler	***Anas clypeata***	NOSH
Northern Pintail	***Anas acuta***	NOPI
Green-winged Teal	***Anas crecca***	GWTE
Canvasback	***Aythya valisineria***	CANV
Redhead	***Aythya americana***	REDH
Ring-necked Duck	***Aythya collaris***	RNDU
Greater Scaup	*Aythya marila*	
Lesser Scaup	***Aythya affinis***	LESC
Bufflehead	***Bucephala albeola***	BUFF
Common Goldeneye	*Bucephala clangula*	COGO
Common Merganser	*Mergus merganser*	COME
Ruddy Duck	***Oxyura jamaicensis***	RUDU
Sharp-tailed Grouse	***Tympanuchus phasianellus***	STGR
Greater Prairie-Chicken	*Tympanuchus cupido*	
Common Loon	*Gavia immer*	
Pied-billed Grebe	***Podilymbus podiceps***	PBGR
Horned Grebe	***Podiceps auritus***	

Common name	Scientific name	Species code
Red-necked Grebe	*Podiceps grisegena*	
Eared Grebe	***Podiceps nigricollis***	EAGR
Western Grebe	***Aechmophorus occidentalis***	WEGR
Clark's Grebe	***Aechmophorus clarkii***	
American White Pelican	*Pelecanus erythrorhynchos*	AWPE
Double-crested Cormorant	***Phalacrocorax auritus***	
American Bittern	***Botaurus lentiginosus***	AMBI
Least Bittern	*Ixobrychus exilis*	
Great Blue Heron	*Ardea herodias*	
Great Egret	***Ardea alba***	
Snowy Egret	***Egretta thula***	
Little Blue Heron	*Egretta caerulea*	
Cattle Egret	***Bubulcus ibis***	
Green Heron	*Butorides virescens*	
Black-crowned Night-Heron	***Nycticorax nycticorax***	BCNH
Yellow-crowned Night-Heron	*Nyctanassa violacea*	
White-faced Ibis	***Plegadis chihi***	
Bald Eagle	*Haliaeetus leucocephalus*	
Northern Harrier	***Circus cyaneus***	NOHA
Swainson's Hawk	***Buteo swainsoni***	
Red-tailed Hawk	***Buteo jamaicensis***	
Ferruginous Hawk	***Buteo regalis***	
Rough-legged Hawk	*Buteo lagopus*	
Golden Eagle	*Aquila chrysaetos*	
Gyrfalcon	*Falco rusticolus*	
Peregrine Falcon	*Falco peregrinus*	
Prairie Falcon	*Falco mexicanus*	
Yellow Rail	***Coturnicops noveboracensis***	
Virginia Rail	***Rallus limicola***	VIRA
Sora	***Porzana carolina***	
American Coot	***Fulica americana***	

Common name	Scientific name	Species code
Sandhill Crane	*Grus canadensis*	
Whooping Crane	*Grus americana*	WHCR
Black-bellied Plover	*Pluvialis squatarola*	
American Golden-Plover	*Pluvialis dominica*	
Semipalmated Plover	*Charadrius semipalmatus*	
Piping Plover	***Charadrius melodus***	**PIPL**
Killdeer	***Charadrius vociferus***	**KILL**
American Avocet	***Recurvirostra americana***	**AMAV**
Greater Yellowlegs	*Tringa melanoleuca*	
Lesser Yellowlegs	*Tringa flavipes*	LEYE
Solitary Sandpiper	*Tringa solitaria*	
Willet	***Catoptrophorus semipalmatus***	**WILL**
Spotted Sandpiper	***Actitis macularia***	**SPSA**
Upland Sandpiper	***Bartramia longicauda***	**UPSA**
Whimbrel	*Numenius phaeopus*	
Long-billed Curlew	*Numenius americanus*	
Hudsonian Godwit	*Limosa haemastica*	
Marbled Godwit	***Limosa fedoa***	**MAGO**
Ruddy Turnstone	*Arenaria interpres*	
Red Knot	*Calidris canutus*	
Sanderling	*Calidris alba*	
Semipalmated Sandpiper	*Calidris pusilla*	SESA
Western Sandpiper	*Calidris mauri*	
Least Sandpiper	*Calidris minutilla*	LESA
White-rumped Sandpiper	*Calidris fuscicollis*	
Baird's Sandpiper	*Calidris bairdii*	BASA
Pectoral Sandpiper	*Calidris melanotos*	
Dunlin	*Calidris alpina*	
Stilt Sandpiper	*Calidris himantopus*	
Buff-breasted Sandpiper	*Tryngites subruficollis*	
Short-billed Dowitcher	*Limnodromus griseus*	

Common name	Scientific name	Species code
Long-billed Dowitcher	*Limnodromus scolopaceus*	LBDO
Wilson's Snipe	***Gallinago delicata***	
Common Snipe	*Gallinago gallinago*	COSN
Wilson's Phalarope	***Phalaropus tricolor***	**WIPH**
Red-necked Phalarope	*Phalaropus lobatus*	
Franklin's Gull	***Larus pipixcan***	**FRGU**
Bonaparte's Gull	*Larus philadelphia*	
Ring-billed Gull	***Larus delawarensis***	
California Gull	*Larus californicus*	
Herring Gull	*Larus argentatus*	
Caspian Tern	*Sterna caspia*	
Common Tern	***Sterna hirundo***	
Forster's Tern	***Sterna forsteri***	**FOTE**
Least Tern	*Sterna antillarum*	LETE
Black Tern	***Chlidonias niger***	**BLTE**
Rock Pigeon	***Columba livia***	
Mourning Dove	***Zenaida macroura***	
Black-billed Cuckoo	***Coccyzus erythropthalmus***	
Yellow-billed Cuckoo	*Coccyzus americanus*	
Snowy Owl	*Bubo scandiacus*	
Burrowing Owl	*Athene cunicularia*	
Long-eared Owl	*Asio otus*	
Long-eared Owl	*Asio otus*	
Short-eared Owl	***Asio flammeus***	**SEOW**
Whip-poor-will	*Caprimulgus vociferus*	
Red-headed Woodpecker	***Melanerpes erythrocephalus***	
Red-bellied Woodpecker	*Melanerpes carolinus*	
Yellow-bellied Sapsucker	*Sphyrapicus varius*	
Olive-sided Flycatcher	*Contopus cooperi*	
Yellow-bellied Flycatcher	*Empidonax flaviventris*	
Willow Flycatcher	***Empidonax traillii***	

Appendix A. (continued)

Common name	Scientific name	Species code
Loggerhead Shrike	*Lanius ludovicianus*	
Northern Shrike	*Lanius excubitor*	
Yellow-throated Vireo	*Vireo flavifrons*	
Blue-headed Vireo	*Vireo solitarius*	
Philadelphia Vireo	*Vireo philadelphicus*	
Horned Lark	*Eremophila alpestris*	HOLA
Winter Wren	*Troglodytes troglodytes*	
Sedge Wren	*Cistothorus platensis*	SEWR
Mountain Bluebird	*Sialia currucoides*	
Brown Thrasher	*Toxostoma rufum*	
Sprague's Pipit	*Anthus spragueii*	SPPI
Bohemian Waxwing	*Bombycilla garrulus*	
Tennessee Warbler	*Vermivora peregrina*	
Nashville Warbler	*Vermivora ruficapilla*	
Chestnut-sided Warbler	*Dendroica pensylvanica*	
Magnolia Warbler	*Dendroica magnolia*	
Cape May Warbler	*Dendroica tigrina*	
Black-throated Green Warbler	*Dendroica virens*	
Blackburnian Warbler	*Dendroica fusca*	
Connecticut Warbler	*Oporornis agilis*	
Mourning Warbler	*Oporornis philadelphia*	
Canada Warbler	*Wilsonia canadensis*	
American Tree Sparrow	*Spizella arborea*	
Clay-colored Sparrow	*Spizella pallida*	CCSP
Lark Bunting	*Calamospiza melanocorys*	LARB
Savannah Sparrow	*Passerculus sandwichensis*	SAVS
Grasshopper Sparrow	*Ammodramus savannarum*	GRSP
Baird's Sparrow	*Ammodramus bairdii*	BAIS
Henslow's Sparrow	*Ammodramus henslowii*	
Le Conte's Sparrow	*Ammodramus leconteii*	
Nelson's Sharp-tailed Sparrow	*Ammodramus nelsoni*	

Common name	Scientific name	Species code
Fox Sparrow	*Passerella iliaca*	
Song Sparrow	***Melospiza melodia***	SOSP
Lincoln's Sparrow	*Melospiza lincolnii*	
Swamp Sparrow	*Melospiza georgiana*	
White-throated Sparrow	*Zonotrichia albicollis*	
Harris's Sparrow	*Zonotrichia querula*	
McCown's Longspur	*Calcarius mccownii*	
Lapland Longspur	*Calcarius lapponicus*	
Smith's Longspur	*Calcarius pictus*	
Chestnut-collared Longspur	***Calcarius ornatus***	CCLO
Snow Bunting	*Plectrophenax nivalis*	
Indigo Bunting	*Passerina cyanea*	
Dickcissel	***Spiza americana***	DICK
Bobolink	***Dolichonyx oryzivorus***	BOBO
Western Meadowlark	***Sturnella neglecta***	WEME
Yellow-headed Blackbird	***Xanthocephalus xanthocephalus***	
Rusty Blackbird	*Euphagus carolinus*	
Pine Grosbeak	*Pinicola enucleator*	
White-winged Crossbill	*Loxia leucoptera*	
Hoary Redpoll	*Carduelis hornemanni*	

Mammals

American badger	*Taxidea taxus*	
Deer mouse	*Peromyscus maniculatus*	
Raccoon	*Procyon lotor*	
Red fox	*Vulpes vulpes*	
Striped skunk	*Mephitis mephitis*	
Masked shrew	*Sorex cinerus*	
Northern short-tailed shrew	*Blarina brevicauda*	
White-footed mouse	*Peromyscus maniculatus*	

Appendix A. (continued)

Common name	Scientific name	Species code
Plants		
Absinth wormwood	*Artemisia vulgaris*	
American watermilfoil	*Myriophyllum sibiricum*	
Blacksamson echinacea	*Echinacea angustifolia*	
Blue grama	*Bouteloua gracilis*	
Blue-green algae	*Merismopedia sp.*	
Bulrush	*Schoenoplectus spp.*	
Canada thistle	*Cirsium arvense*	
Cattail	*Typha spp.*	
Cocklebur	*Xanthium sp.*	
Common bladderwort	*Utricularia macrorhiza*	
Common reed	*Phragmites australis*	
Common spikerush	*Eleocharis palustris*	
Cosmopolitan bulrush	*Schoenoplectus maritimus*	
Crested wheatgrass	*Agropyron cristatum*	
Dock	*Rumex sp.*	
Fendler threeawn	*Aristida purpurea*	
Flatspine stickseed	*Lappula occidentalis*	
Foxtail barley	*Hordeum jubatum*	
Grama	*Bouteloua spp.*	
Green needlegrass	*Nassella viridula*	
Kentucky bluegrass	*Poa pratensis*	
Kochia	*Kochia sp.*	
Leafy spurge	*Euphorbia esula*	
Little bluestem	*Schizachyrium scoparium*	
Lotus milkvetch	*Astragalus lotiflorus*	
Muskgrass	*Chara spp.*	
Narrow-leaved cattail	*Typha angustifolia*	
Narrowleaf goosefoot	*Chenopodium leptophyllum*	
Needle-and-thread	*Hesperostipa comata*	
Needleleaf sedge	*Carex duriuscula*	

Common name	Scientific name	Species code
Nuttall's alkaligrass	*Puccinellia nuttalliana*	
Pondweed	*Potamogeton spp.*	
Porcupine grass	*Hesperostipa spartea*	
Prairie cordgrass	*Spartina pectinata*	
Prairie junegrass	*Koeleria macrantha*	
Prairie sagewort, fringed sage	*Artemisia frigida*	
Prairie sandreed	*Calamovilfa longifolia*	
Purple prairie clover	*Dalea lasiathera*	
Reed canary grass	*Phalaris arundinacea*	
Russian olive	*Elaeagnus angustifolia*	
Sago pondweed	*Stuckenia pectinatus*	
Saltgrass (inland)	*Distichlis spicata*	
Sandberg bluegrass	*Poa secunda*	
Scarlet beeblossom	*Gaura coccinea*	
Seaside arrowgrass	*Triglochin maritimum*	
Sedge	*Carex spp.*	
Seepweed	*Suaeda sp.*	
Sideoats grama	*Bouteloua curtipendula*	
Slender wheatgrass	*Elymus trachycaulus*	
Smartweed	*Polygonum spp.*	
Smooth brome	*Bromus inermis*	
Softstem bulrush	*Schoenoplectus tabernaemontani*	
Spikerush	*Eleocharis sp.*	
Spike watermilfoil	*Myriophyllum spicatum*	
Spiny phlox	*Phlox hoodii*	
Sprangletop	*Scolochloa festucacea*	
Stiffstem flax	*Linum rigidum*	
Sun sedge	*Carex inops*	
Sweet clover	*Melilotus spp.*	
Switchgrass	*Panicum virgatum*	
Tarragon	*Artemisia dracunculus*	

Appendix A. (continued)

Common name	Scientific name	Species code
Threadleaf sedge	*Carex filifolia*	
Three-square bulrush	*Schoenoplectus americanus*	
Tule bulrush	*Schoenoplectus acutis*	
Western wheatgrass	*Pascopyrum smithii*	
White milkwort	*Polygala alba*	
White sagebrush, white sage	*Artemisia ludoviciana*	
Widgeon grass	*Ruppia maritima*	
Woolly plantain	*Plantago patagonica*	

[a] Integrated Taxonomic Information System. 2004. U.S. Department of Agriculture, National Oceanic and Atmospheric Administration, U.S. Geological Survey, Smithsonian Institution, U.S. Environmental Protection Agency, NatureServe, U.S. National Park Service, Agriculture and Agri-Food Canada. <http://www.itis.usda.gov> (17 January 2005)

Appendix B. Conservation status of avian species known to occur on the Long Lake National Wildlife Refuge Complex based on various regional and national plans. Species listed in Birds of Conservation Concern are denoted with an "X", whereas species listed in the North American Landbird Conservation Plan as Stewardship or Watch species in the Prairie Avifaunal Biome are denoted with an "R" and those species of continental importance are denoted with an "N". Designations listed in the Shorebird Plan are as follows: C- = species of concern; B, M, W = region is highly important to population for breeding, migrating, and wintering, respectively; b, m, w = region is less important to breeding, migrating, wintering shorebirds. Population numbers listed under the North American Waterfowl Management Plan represent population objectives for the mid-continent region (K = thousands, M = millions).

Species	Birds of Conservation Concern 2002			North American Landbird Conservation Plan		Northern Plains and Prairie Pothole Region Shorebird Plan	North American Waterfowl Management Plan	North American Waterbird Management Plan Conservation Concern
	BCR 11	Region 6	National	Watch	Steward			
Geese, Swans, Ducks								
Greater White-fronted Goose							600.0 K	
Snow Goose							1.0 M	
Trumpeter Swan							2.5 K	
Tundra Swan							80.0 K	
Gadwall							1.5 M	
American Wigeon							3.0 M	
Mallard							8.2 M	
Blue-winged Teal } Cinnamon Teal							4.7 M	
Northern Shoveler							2.0 M	
Northern Pintail							5.6 M	
Green-winged Teal							1.9 M	
Canvasback							540.0 K	
Redhead							640.0 K	
Greater Scaup } Lesser Scaup							6.3 M	
Gallinaceous Birds								
Sharp-tailed Grouse					R, N			
Greater Prairie-Chicken				R, N				
Loons								
Common Loon								Low risk
Grebes								
Pied-billed Grebe								Low risk
Horned Grebe								High concern
Red-necked Grebe								Low risk
Eared Grebe								Moderate concern
Western Grebe								High concern
Clark's Grebe								Low risk
Pelicans, Cormorants								
American White Pelican								Moderate concern
Double-Crested Cormorant								Low risk
Bitterns, Herons, Egrets								
American Bittern	X							High concern
Least Bittern								Listed
Great Blue Heron								Moderate concern
Great Egret								Low risk
Snowy Egret								Low risk
Little Blue Heron		X						Low risk
Cattle Egret								Low risk
Green Heron								Low risk
Black-crowned Night-Heron								Moderate concern
Yellow-crowned Night-Heron								Low risk

Species	Birds of Conservation Concern 2002			North American Landbird Conservation Plan		Northern Plains and Prairie Pothole Region Shorebird Plan	North American Waterfowl Management Plan	North American Waterbird Management Plan Conservation Concern
	BCR 11	Region 6	National	Watch	Steward			
Ibises, Spoonbills								
White-faced Ibis								Low risk
Osprey, Kites, Hawks, Eagles								
Bald Eagle					N			
Northern Harrier	X	X	X					
Swainson's Hawk	X	X	X	R, N				
Ferruginous Hawk	X	X	X					
Rough-legged Hawk					N			
Golden Eagle		X						
Falcons, Caracaras								
Gyrfalcon					N			
Peregrine Falcon	X	X	X		N			
Prairie Falcon		X	X					
Rails								
Yellow Rail	X	X	X					High concern
Virginia Rail								Moderate concern
Sora								Low risk
American Coot								Low risk
Cranes								
Sandhill Crane								Low risk
Whooping Crane								Listed
Plovers								
Black-bellied Plover						M		
American Golden-Plover		X	X			M		
Semipalmated Plover						M		
Piping Plover						C - BM		
Killdeer						BM		
Stilts, Avocets								
American Avocet						C - BM		
Sandpipers, Phalaropes								
Greater Yellowlegs						M		
Lesser Yellowlegs						M		
Solitary Sandpiper	X	X	X			M		
Willet	X					BM		
Spotted Sandpiper						BM		
Upland Sandpiper	X	X	X			C - BM		
Whimbrel			X			m		
Long-billed Curlew	X	X	X			BM		
Hudsonian Godwit	X		X			C - M		
Marbled Godwit	X	X	X			C - BM		
Ruddy Turnstone						M		
Red Knot			X			m		
Sanderling	X					m		
Semipalmated Sandpiper						M		
Western Sandpiper						m		
Least Sandpiper						M		
White-rumped Sandpiper	X					M		
Baird's Sandpiper						M		
Pectoral Sandpiper						M		
Dunlin						M		
Stilt Sandpiper			X			M		
Buff-breasted Sandpiper	X	X	X			M		
Short-billed Dowitcher			X			M		
Long-billed Dowitcher						M		
Wilson's Snipe						bM		
Wilson's Phalarope	X	X	X			C - BM		
Red-necked Phalarope						M		

Species	Birds of Conservation Concern 2002			North American Landbird Conservation Plan		Northern Plains and Prairie Pothole Region Shorebird Plan	North American Waterfowl Management Plan	North American Waterbird Management Plan Conservation Concern
	BCR 11	Region 6	National	Watch	Steward			
Skuas, Jaegers, Gulls, Terns								
Franklin's Gull								High concern
Bonaparte's Gull								Low risk
Ring-billed Gull								Low risk
California Gull								Low risk
Herring Gull								Low risk
Caspian Tern								Moderate concern
Common Tern								Moderate concern
Forster's Tern								Low risk
Least Tern			X					Listed
Black Tern								High concern
Cuckoos, Anis								
Black-billed Cuckoo	X	X	X					
Yellow-billed Cuckoo			X					
Owls								
Snowy Owl						N		
Burrowing Owl	X	X	X					
Long-eared Owl			X					
Short-eared Owl	X	X				R, N		
Nightjars								
Whip-poor-will			X					
Woodpeckers								
Red-headed Woodpecker	X	X	X			R, N		
Red-bellied Woodpecker						N		
Yellow-bellied Sapsucker						N		
Tyrant Flycatchers								
Olive-sided Flycatcher			X			N		
Yellow-bellied Flycatcher						N		
Willow Flycatcher						R, N		
Shrikes								
Loggerhead Shrike	X	X	X					
Northern Shrike						N		
Vireos								
Yellow-throated Vireo						N		
Blue-headed Vireo						N		
Philadelphia Vireo						N		
Larks								
Horned Lark			X					
Wrens								
Winter Wren						N		
Sedge Wren			X					
Thrushes								
Mountain Bluebird						N		
Mimic Thrushes								
Brown Thrasher						N		
Wagtails, Pipits								
Sprague's Pipit	X	X	X	R, N				
Waxwings								
Bohemian Waxwing						N		
Wood Warblers								
Tennessee Warbler						N		
Nashville Warbler						N		
Chestnut-sided Warbler						N		
Magnolia Warbler						N		
Cape May Warbler						N		
Black-throated Green								

Species	Birds of Conservation Concern 2002			North American Landbird Conservation Plan		Northern Plains and Prairie Pothole Region Shorebird Plan	North American Waterfowl Management Plan	North American Waterbird Management Plan Conservation Concern
	BCR 11	Region 6	National	Watch	Steward			
Warbler					N			
Blackburnian Warbler					N			
Connecticut Warbler					N			
Mourning Warbler					N			
Canada Warbler			X		N			
Grosbeaks, Buntings, Sparrows								
American Tree Sparrow					R, N			
Lark Bunting					R, N			
Grasshopper Sparrow	X	X	X		R, N			
Baird's Sparrow	X	X	X	R, N				
Henslow's sparrow	X	X	X	R, N				
Le Conte's Sparrow	X	X	X					
Nelson's Sharp-tailed Sparrow	X	X	X	R, N				
Fox Sparrow					N			
Lincoln's Sparrow					N			
Swamp Sparrow					N			
White-throated Sparrow					N			
Harris's Sparrow			X	R, N				
McCown's Longspur	X	X	X	R, N				
Lapland Longspur					R, N			
Smith's Longspur			X	R, N				
Chestnut-collared Longspur	X	X	X		R, N			
Snow Bunting					N			
Cardinals, Grosbeaks, Allies								
Indigo Bunting					N			
Dickcissel		X	X	R, N				
Blackbirds, Orioles, Finches								
Bobolink		X						
Yellow-headed Blackbird					N			
Rusty Blackbird				R, N				
Pine Grosbeak					N			
White-winged Crossbill					N			
Hoary Redpoll					N			

Appendix C. Quantitative measurements of habitat structure reported in the literature that may be related to use by select avian species: (a) vegetation height at nest sites or within breeding territories of wetland nesting species, (b) water depth at nest sites or within breeding territories of wetland nesting species, (c) water depth at foraging sites, (d) visual obstruction at nest sites or within breeding territories of upland nesting species, (e) vegetation height at nest sites or within breeding territories of upland nesting species, and (f) litter depth at nest sites or within breeding territories of upland nesting species. Species names corresponding to codes are provided in Appendix A.

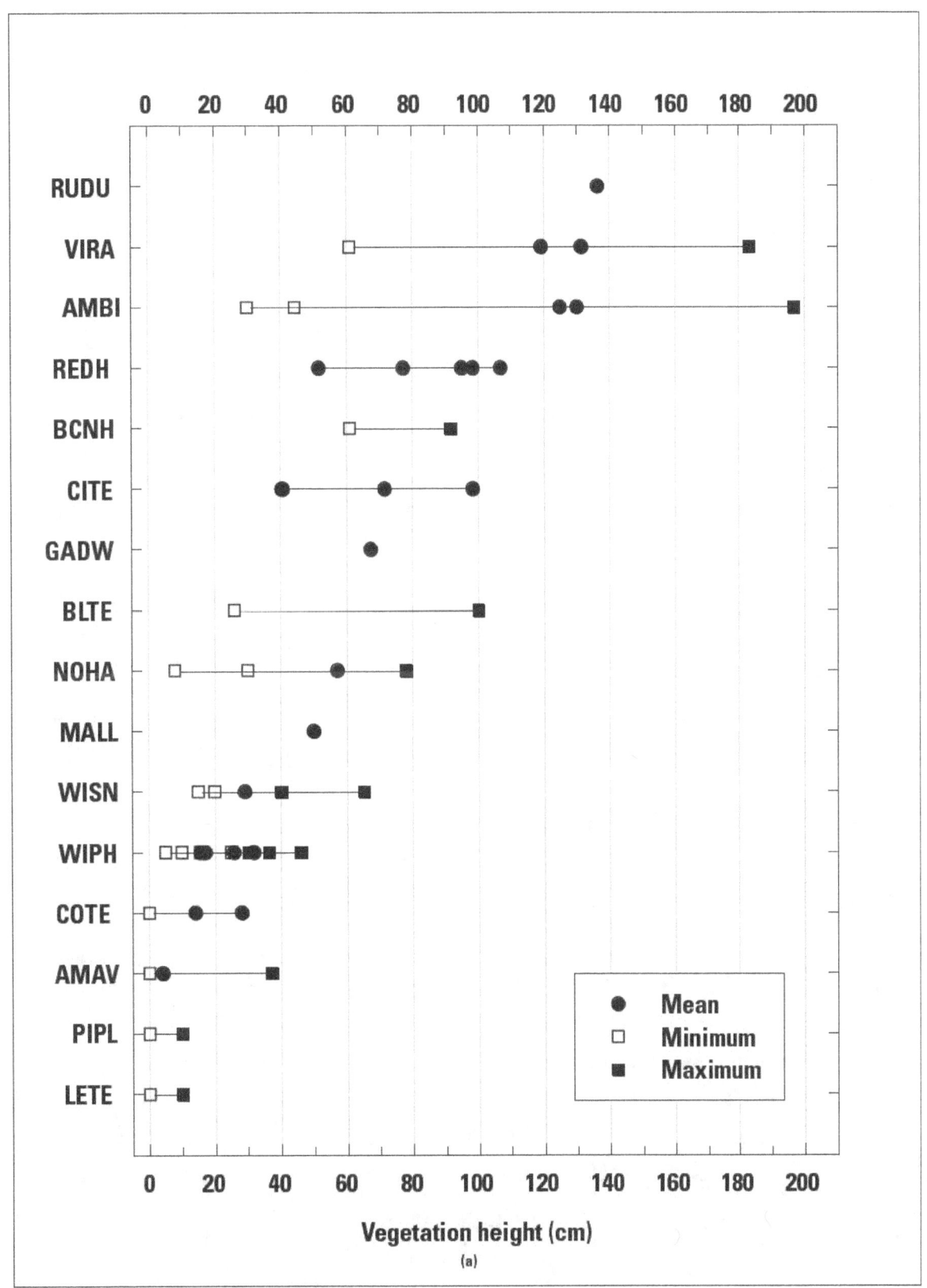

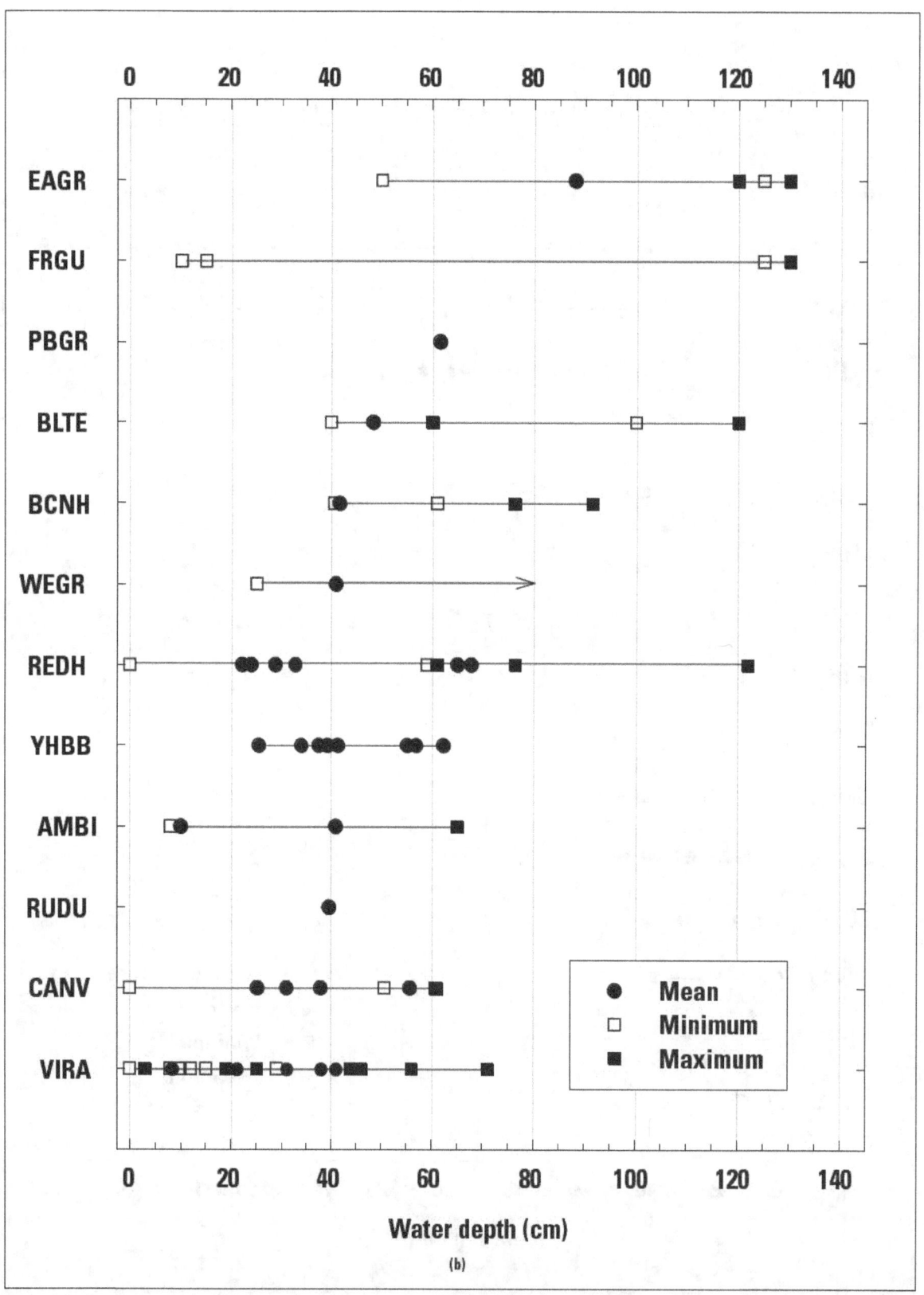

Water depth (cm)

(b)

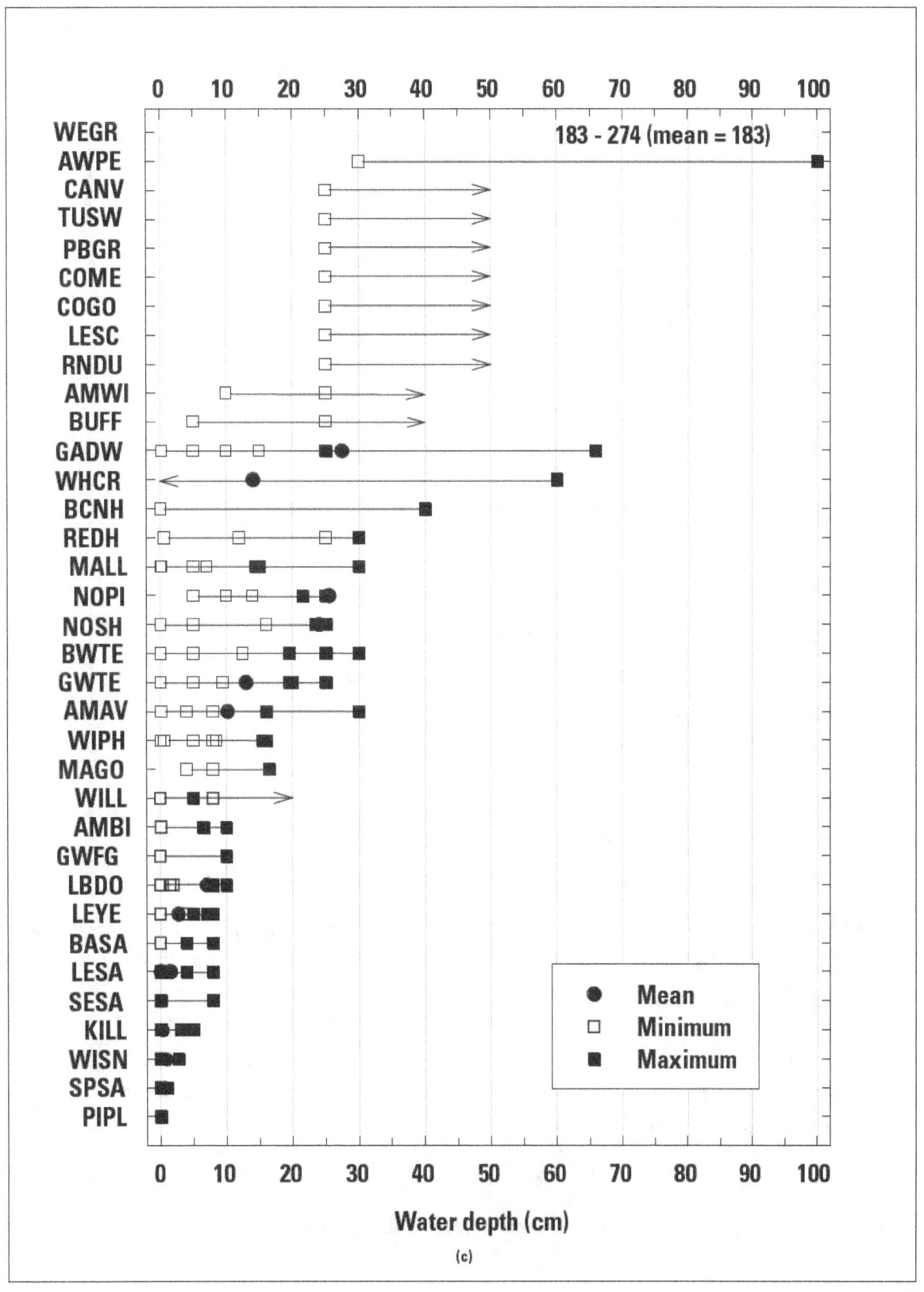

(c)

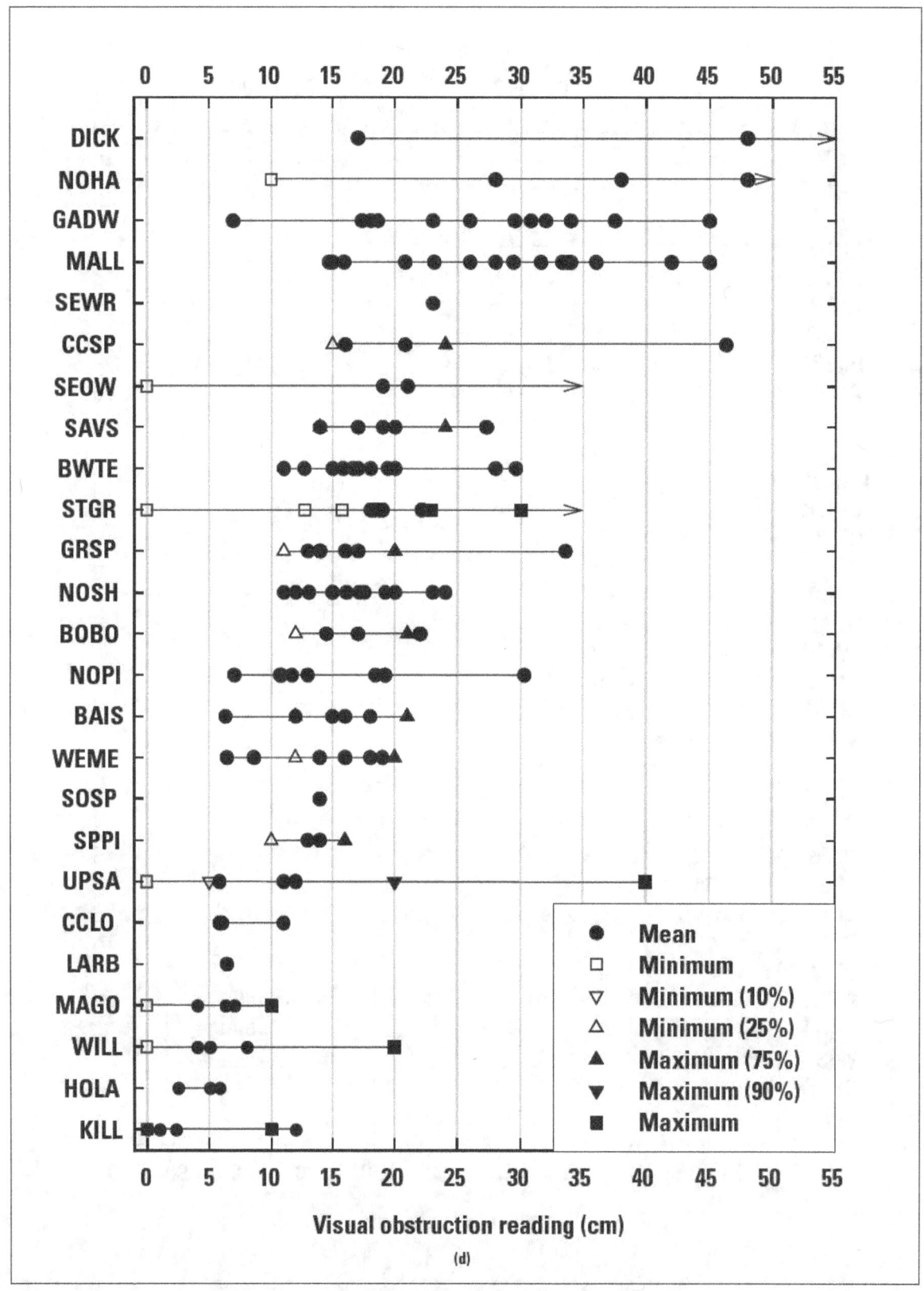

Visual obstruction reading (cm)

(d)

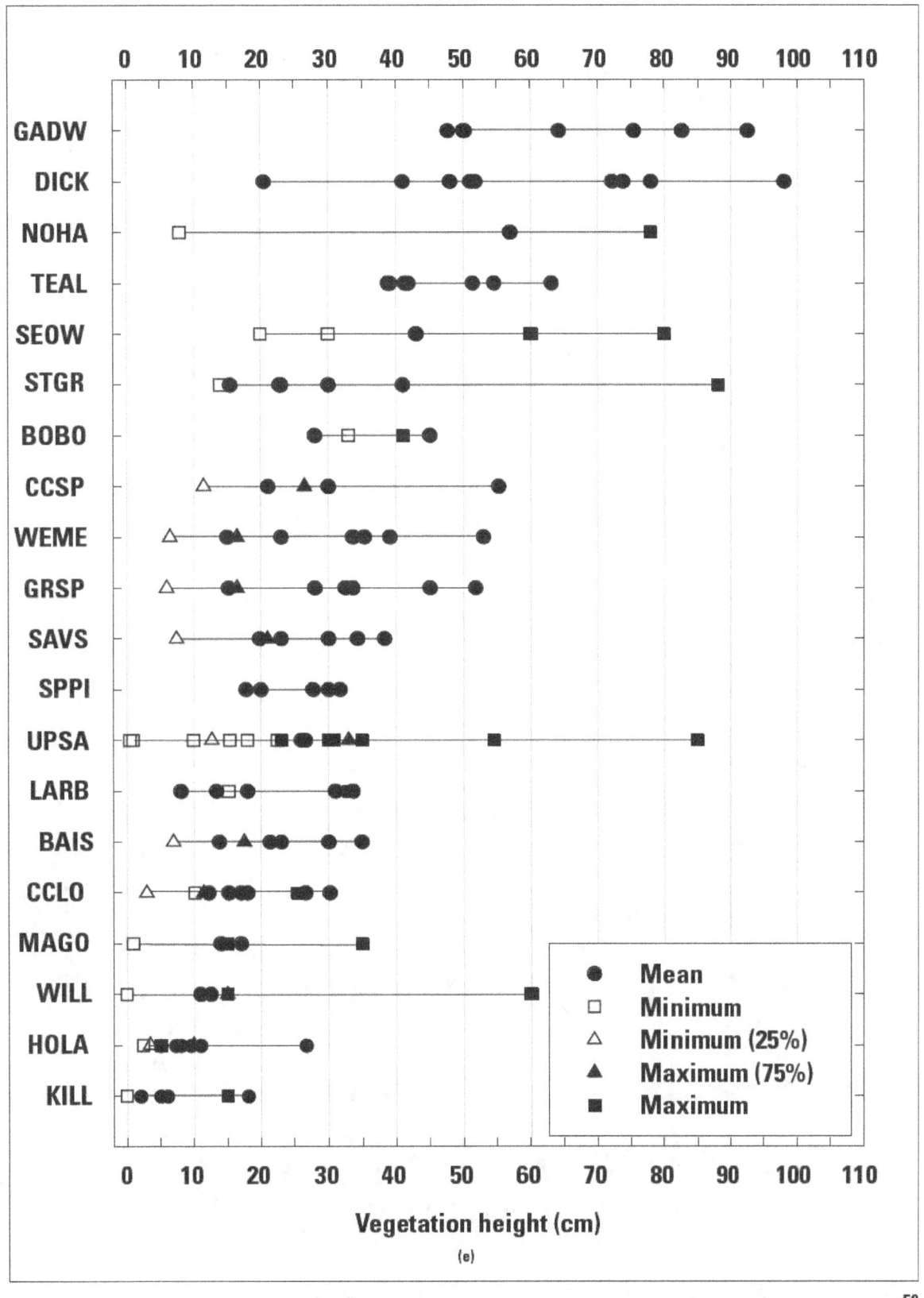

Vegetation height (cm)

(e)

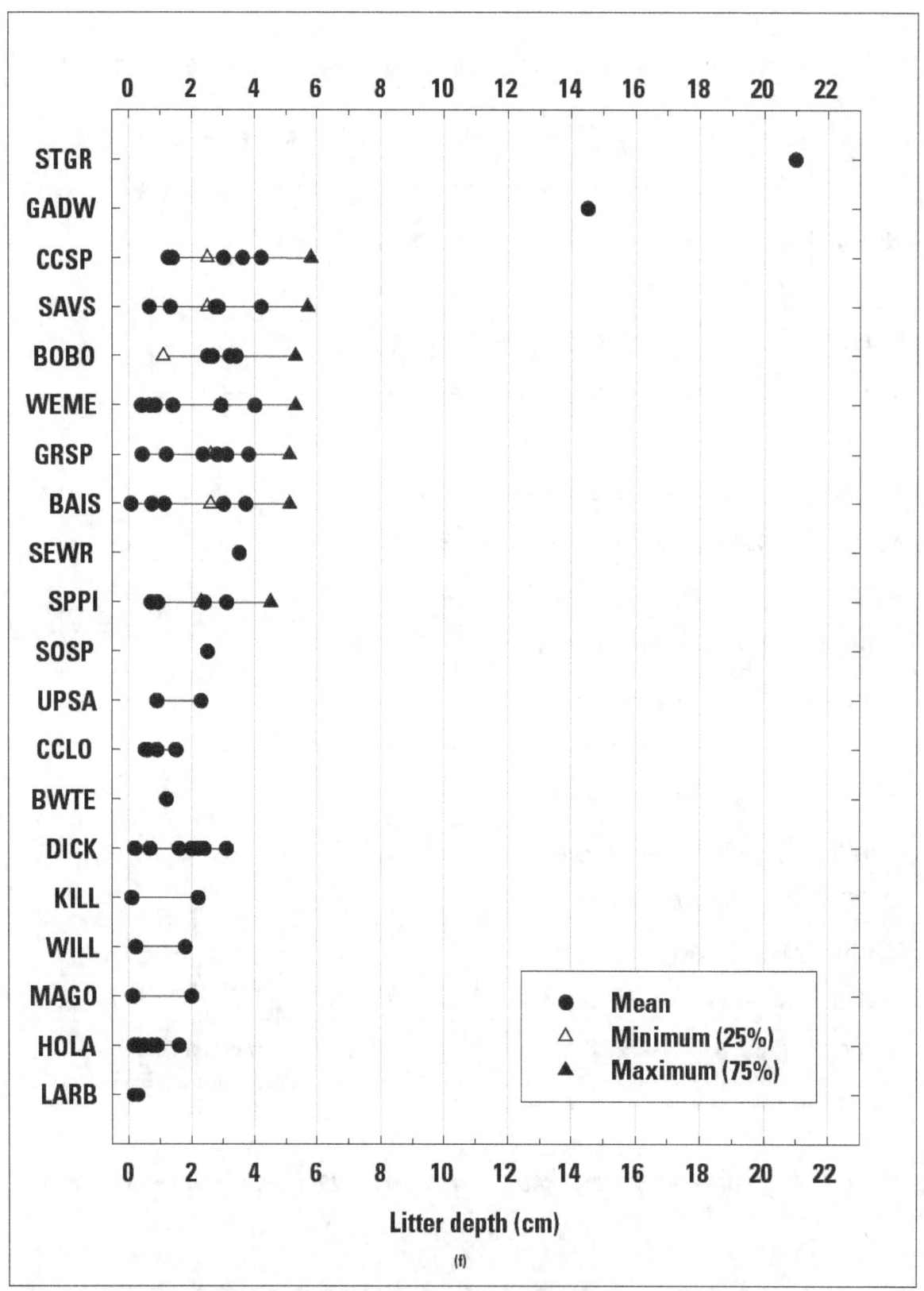

Litter depth (cm)

(f)

Literature Cited

Anderson, J. G. T. 1991. Foraging behavior of the American white pelican (*Pelecanus erythrorhyncos*) in western Nevada. Colonial Waterbirds 14:166-172.

Baldassarre, G. A., and D. H. Fischer. 1984. Food habits of fall migrant shorebirds on the Texas High Plains. Journal of Field Ornithology 55:220-229.

Baldwin, P. H., J. D. Butterfield, P. D. Creighton, and R. Shook. 1969. Summer ecology of the lark bunting. U.S. International Biological Program, Grassland Biome Technical Report Number 29. Colorado State University, Fort Collins, CO.

Boe, J. S. 1993. Colony site selection by eared grebes in Minnesota. Colonial Waterbirds 16:28-38.

Bolster, D. C. 1990. Habitat use by the upland sandpiper in northeastern Colorado. M.S. thesis, University of Colorado, Boulder, CO.

Bomberger, L. 1984. Quantitative assessment of the nesting habitat of Wilson's Phalarope. Wilson Bulletin 96:126-128.

Bowen, B. S., and A. D. Kruse. 1993. Effects of grazing on nesting by upland sandpipers in southcentral North Dakota. Journal of Wildlife Management 57:291-301.

Brininger, W. L., Jr. 1996. The ecology of the American bittern in northwest Minnesota. M.A. thesis, St. Cloud University, St. Cloud, MN.

Brua, R. B. 1999. Ruddy duck nesting success: do nest characteristics deter nest predation? Condor 101:867-870.

Burger, J., and M. Gochfeld. 1988. Nest-site selection and temporal patterns in habitat use of Roseate and Common terns. Auk 105:433-438.

Burger, J., and M. Gochfeld. 1994. Franklin's gull (*Larus pipixcan*). In A. Poole and F. Gill [eds]. The Birds of North America, No. 116. Academy of Natural Sciences, Philadelphia, Pennsylvania; American Ornithologist' Union, Washington, DC.

Burger, J., and M. Gochfeld. 1995. Nest site selection by Eared Grebes in a Franklin's Gull colony: structural stability parasites. Condor 97:577-580.

Colwell, M. A., and L. W. Oring. 1990. Nest site characteristics of prairie shorebirds. Canadian Journal of Zoology 68:297-302.

Crabtree, R. L., L. S. Broome, and M. L. Wolfe. 1989. Effects of habitat characteristics on gadwall nest predation and nest-site selection. Journal of Wildlife Management 53:129-137.

Creighton, P. D., and P. H. Baldwin. 1974. Habitat exploitation by an avian ground-foraging guild. U.S. International Biological Program, Grassland Biome Technical Report Number 263. Colorado State University, Fort Collins, CO.

Custer, C. M. 1993. Life history traits and habitat needs of the redhead. U.S. Fish and Wildlife Service, Waterfowl Management Handbook, Fish and Wildlife Leaflet 13.1.11, Washington, DC.

Dale, B. C. 1983. Habitat relationships of seven species of passerine birds at Last Mountain Lake, Saskatchewan. M.S. thesis, University of Regina, Regina, SASK.

Delisle, J. M., and J. A. Savidge. 1997. Avian use and vegetation characteristics of Conservation Reserve Program fields. Journal of Wildlife Management 61:318-325.

Dieni, J. S., and S. L. Jones. 2003. Grassland songbird nest site selection patterns in northcentral Montana. Wilson Bulletin 115:388-396.

Dirks, B., M. Schwalbach, K. F. Higgins, and C. Kruse. 1993. Soil substrates, objects, and vegetation at piping plover and interior least tern nest sites in South Dakota, p. 93-94. In K. F. Higgins and M. R. Brashier [eds.], Proceedings of the Missouri River and its tributaries: piping plover and least tern symposium. South Dakota State University, Brookings, SD.

Dole, D. A. 1986. Nesting and foraging behavior of American avocets. M.A. thesis, University of Montana, Missoula, MT.

Dorio, J. C., and A. H. Grewe. 1979. Nesting and brood rearing habitat for the upland sandpiper. Minnesota Academy of Science 45:8-11.

DuBowy, P. J. 1988. Waterfowl communities and seasonal environments: temporal variability in interspecific competition. Ecology 69:1439-1453.

Duebbert, H. F., and J. T. Lokemoen. 1977. Upland nesting of American bitterns, marsh hawks, and short-eared owls. Prairie Naturalist 9:33-40.

Duebbert, H. F., J. T. Lokemoen, and D. E. Sharp. 1986. Nest sites of ducks in grazed mixed-grass prairie in North Dakota. Prairie Naturalist 18:99-108.

Du Mont, P. A. 1940. Relation of the Franklin's gull colonies to agriculture in the Great Plains. Transactions of the North American Wildlife Conference 5:183-189.

Dunn, E. H. 1979. Nesting biology and development of young in Ontario black terns. Canadian Field-Naturalist 93:276-281.

Eldridge, J. 1992. Management of habitat for breeding and migrating shorebirds in the midwest. U.S. Fish and Wildlife Service, Waterfowl Management Handbook, Fish and Wildlife Leaflet 13.2.14, Washington, DC.

Featherstone, J. D. 1975. Aspects of nest site selection in three species of ducks. Ph.D. dissertation. University of Toronto, ONT.

Fitcher, S. C., M. A. Rumble, and L. D. Flake. 2004. Grassland bird densities in seral stages of mixed-grass prairie. Journal of Range Management 57:351-357.

Fleskes, J. P., and E. E. Klaas. 1991. Dabbling duck recruitment in relation to habitat and predators at Union Slough National Wildlife Refuge, Iowa. U.S. Fish and Wildlife Service, Fish and Wildlife Technical Report 32. Washington, DC.

Fondell, T. F., and I. J. Ball. 2004. Density and success of bird nests relative to grazing on western Montana grasslands. Biological Conservation 117:203-213.

Frawley, B. J., and L. B. Best. 1991. Effects of mowing on breeding bird abundance and species composition in alfalfa fields. Wildlife Society Bulletin 19:135-142.

Fredrickson, L. H. 1991. Strategies for water level manipulations in moist-soil systems. U.S. Fish and Wildlife Service, Waterfowl Management Handbook, Fish and Wildlife Leaflet 13.4.6, Washington, DC.

Fredrickson, L. H., and M. K. Laubhan. 1994. Managing wetlands for wildlife, p. 623-647. In T. A. Bookhout [ed.], Research and management techniques for wildlife and habitats. 5th ed. The Wildlife Society, Besthesda, MD.

Fredrickson, L. H., and F. A. Reid. 1986. Wetland and riparian habitats: a nongame overview, p. 58-96. In J.B. Hale, L. B. Best, and R. L. Clawson [eds.], Management of nongame wildlife in the midwest: a developing art. Proceedings of the 47th Midwest Fish and Wildlife Conference, North Central Section, The Wildlife Society, Grand Rapids, MI.

Fredrickson, L. H. 1988. Waterfowl use of wetland complexes. U.S. Fish and Wildlife Service, Waterfowl Management Handbook, Fish and Wildlife Leaflet 13.2.1, Washington, DC.

Fredrickson, L. H., and M. W. Sayre. 1983. Factors influencing production and utilization of moist-soil foods, p. 24-26. In H. H. Allen and L. R. Aggus [eds.], Effects of fluctuating reservoir water levels on fisheries, wildlife, and vegetation. Miscellaneous Paper E-83-2, U.S. Army of Engineer Waterways Experiment Station, Vicksburg, MI.

Giezentanner, J. B. 1970a. Avian distribution and population fluctuations on the shortgrass prairie in north central Colorado. M.S. thesis, Colorado State University, Fort Collins, CO.

Giezentanner, J. B. 1970b. Avian distribution and population fluctuations at the Pawnee site. U.S. International Biological Program, Grassland Biome Technical Report Number 28. Colorado State University, Fort Collins, CO.

Glover, F. A. 1953. Nesting ecology of the Pied-billed Grebe in northwestern Iowa. Wilson Bulletin 65:32-39.

Griese, H. J., R. A. Ryder, and C. E. Braun. 1980. Spatial and temporal distribution of rails in Colorado. Wilson Bulletin 92:96-102.

Grosz, K. L. 1988. Sharp-tailed grouse nesting and brood rearing habitat in grazed and nongrazed treatments in southcentral North Dakota. M.S. thesis, North Dakota State University, Fargo, ND.

Hanowski, J. M., and G. J. Niemi. 1986. Habitat characteristics for bird species of special concern. Unpublished report to Minnesota Department of Natural Resources, St. Paul, MN.

Helmers, D. L. 1992. Shorebird management manual. Western Hemisphere Shorebird Reserve Network, Manomet, MA.

Hertel, D. R. 1987. Effects of grazing systems on habitats used by upland nesting waterfowl in south central North Dakota. M.S. thesis, North Dakota State University, Fargo, ND.

Hickey, J. M., and R. A. Malecki. 1997. Nest site selection of the black tern in western New York. Colonial Waterbirds 20:582-595.

Higgins, K. F., L. M. Kirsch, M. R. Ryan, and R. B. Renken. 1979. Some ecological aspects of marbled godwits and willets in North Dakota. Prairie Naturalist 11:115-118.

Holm, J. W. 1984. Nest success and cover relationships of upland-nesting ducks in north central Montana. M.S. thesis, University of Montana, Missoula, MT.

Horak, G. J. 1964. A comparative study of Virginia and sora rails with emphasis on foods. M.S. thesis, Iowa State University, Ames, IA.

Howe, M. A. 1989. Migration of radio-marked whooping cranes from the Aransas-Wood Buffalo population: patterns of habitat use, behavior, and survival. U.S. Fish and Wildlife Service, Fish and Wildlife Technical Report 21, Washington, DC.

Hughes, J. P. 1996. The effect of vegetative structure and landscape composition on avian abundance and reproductive success in CRP fields in northeastern Kansas. M.S. thesis, Kansas State University, Manhattan, KS.

Jensen, W. E. 1999. Nesting habitat and responses to habitat edges of three grassland passerine species. M.S. thesis, Emporia State University, Emporia, KS.

Johnson, B. R., and R. R. Ryder. 1977. Breeding densities and migration periods of Common Snipe in Colorado. Wilson Bulletin 89:116-121.

Johnson, R. R., and J. J. Dinsmore. 1986. Habitat use by breeding Virginia rails and soras. Journal of Wildlife Management 50:387-392.

Joyner, D. E. 1978. Use of an old field habitat by bobolinks and red-winged blackbirds. Canadian Field-Naturalist 92:383-386.

Kaiser, P. H. 1979. Upland sandpiper nesting in southeastern South Dakota. Proceedings of the South Dakota Academy of Science 58:59-68.

Kantrud, H. A., and K. F. Higgins. 1992. Nest and nest site characteristics of some ground-nesting, non-passerine birds of northern grasslands. Prairie Naturalist 24:67-84.

Kantrud, H. A., and R. L. Kologiski. 1982. Effects of soils and grazing on breeding birds of uncultivated upland grasslands of the northern Great Plains. U.S. Fish and Wildlife Service, Wildlife Research Report 15, Washington, DC.

Kirsch, L. M., and K. F. Higgins. 1976. Upland sandpiper nesting and management in North Dakota. Wildlife Society Bulletin 4:16-20.

Knopf, F. L., and J. L. Kennedy. 1980. Foraging sites of white pelicans nesting at Pyramid Lake, Nevada. Western Birds 11:175-180.

Kohn, S. C. 1982. Sharp-tailed grouse nesting habitat in southwestern North Dakota. Proceedings of the Wildlife-Livestock Relationships Symposium 10:166-174.

Krapu, G. L., and H. F. Duebbert. 1974. A biological survey of Kraft Slough. Prairie Naturalist 6:33-55.

Kruse, A. D., and B. S. Bowen. 1996. Effects of grazing and burning on densities and habitats of breeding ducks in North Dakota. Journal of Wildlife Management 60:233-246.

Laubhan, M. K., and J. H. Gammonley. 2000. Density and foraging habitat selection of waterbirds breeding in the San Luis Valley of Colorado. Journal of Wildlife Management 64:808-819.

Lawrence, G. E. 1950. The diving and feeding activity of the Western Grebe on the breeding grounds. Condor 52:3-16.

Lindmeier, J. P. 1960. Plover, rail, and godwit nesting on a study area in Mahhonen County, Minnesota. Flicker 32:5-9.

Lokemoen, J. T. 1966. Breeding ecology of the redhead duck in western Montana. Journal of Wildlife Management 30:668-681.

Lokemoen, J. T., H. F. Duebbert, and D. E. Sharp. 1984. Nest spacing, habitat selection, and behavior of waterfowl on Miller Lake Island, North Dakota. Journal of Wildlife Management 48:309-321.

Lovvorn, J. R., and M. P. Gillingham. 1996. Food dispersion and foraging energetics: a mechanistic synthesis for field studies of avian benthivores. Ecology 77:435-451.

Madden, E. M. 1996. Passerine communities and bird-habitat relationships on prescribe-burned, mixed prairie in North Dakota. M.S. thesis, Montana State University, Bozeman, MT.

Maxson, S. J., and M. R. Riggs. 1996. Habitat use and nest success of overwater nesting ducks in westcentral Minnesota. Journal of Wildlife Management 60:108-119.

McMahon, B. F., and R. M. Evans. 1985. Nocturnal foraging in the American white pelican. Condor 94:101-109.

McMaster, D. G., and S. K. Davis. 2001. An evaluation of Canada's Permanent Cover Program: habitat for grassland birds? Journal of Field Ornithology 72:195-210.

Nenneman, M. P. 2003. Vegetation structure and floristics at nest sites of grassland birds in north central North Dakota. M.S. thesis, University of Montana, Missoula, MT.

Nickell, W. P. 1966. The nesting of the black-crowned night heron and its associates. Jack Pine Warbler 44:130-139.

Nielsen, L. S., and C. A. Yde. 1982. The effects of rest-rotation grazing on the distribution of sharp-tailed grouse. Proceedings of the Wildlife-Livestock Relationships Symposium 10:147-165.

Nuechterlein, G. L. 1975. Nesting ecology of western grebes on the Delta Marsh, Manitoba. M.S. thesis, Colorado State University, Fort Collins, CO.

Patterson, M. P., and L. B. Best. 1996. Bird abundance and nesting success in Iowa CRP fields: the importance of vegetation structure and composition. American Midland Naturalist 135:153-167.

Posphical, L. B., and W. H. Marshall. 1954. A field study of sora rail and Virginia rail in central Minnesota. Flicker 26:2-32.

Provost, M. W. 1947. Nesting of birds in marshes of northwest Iowa. American Midland Naturalist 38:485-503.

Renken, R. B. 1983. Breeding bird communities and bird-habitat associations on North Dakota Waterfowl Production Areas of three habitat types. M.S. thesis, Iowa State University, Ames, IA.

Ringelman, J. K. 1990. Life history traits and management of the gadwall. U.S. Fish and Wildlife Service, Waterfowl Management Handbook, Fish and Wildlife Leaflet 13.1.2, Washington, DC.

Rundle, W. D., and L. H. Fredrickson. 1981. Managing seasonally flooded impoundments for migrant rails and shorebirds. Wildlife Society Bulletin 9:80-87.

Ryan, M. R. 1982. Marbled godwit habitat selection in the northern prairie region. Ph.D. dissertation, Iowa State University, Ames, IA.

Ryan, M. R., and R. B. Renken. 1987. Habitat use by breeding willets in the northern Great Plains. Wilson Bulletin 99:175-189.

Ryan, M. R., R. B. Renken, and J. J. Dinsmore. 1984. Marbled godwit habitat selection in the northern prairie region. Journal of Wildlife Management 48:1206-1218.

Safran, R. J., C. R. Isola, M. A. Colwell, and O. E. Williams. 1997. Benthic invertebrates at foraging locations of nine waterbird species in managed wetlands of the northern San Joaquin Valley, California. Wetlands 17:407-415.

Scheiman, D. M., E. K. Bollinger, and D. H. Johnson. 2003. Effects of leafy spurge infestation on grassland birds. Journal of Wildlife Management 67:115-121.

Sedivec, K. K. 1994. Grazing treatment effects on and habitat use of upland nesting birds on native rangeland. Ph.D. dissertation, North Dakota State University, Fargo, ND.

Shane, T. G. 1972. The nest-site selection behavior of the lark bunting, *Calamospiza melanocorys*. M.S. thesis, Kansas State University, Manhattan, KS.

Sidle, J. G., and P. M. Arnold. 1982. Nesting of American avocet in North Dakota. Prairie Naturalist 14:73-80.

Sisson, L. 1976. The sharp-tailed grouse in Nebraska. Nebraska Game and Parks Commission, Lincoln, NE.

Skagen, S. K., and F. L. Knopf. 1994. Migrating shorebirds and habitat dynamics at a prairie wetland complex. Wilson Bulletin 106:91-105.

Smith, H., and J. Smith. 1966. A breeding bird survey on uncultivated grassland at Regina. Blue Jay 24:129-131.

Stewart, R. E. 1975. Breeding birds of North Dakota. Tri-College Center for Environmental Studies, Fargo, ND.

Stoudt, J. H. 1982. Habitat use and productivity of canvasbacks in southwestern Manitoba, 1961-1972. U.S. Fish and Wildlife Service, Special Scientific Report 248, Washington, DC.

Sutter, G. C. 1996. Habitat selection and prairie drought in relation to grassland bird community structure and the nesting ecology of Sprague's pipit, *Anthus spragueii*. Ph.D. dissertation, University of Regina, Regina, SASK.

Sutter, G. C. 1997. Nest-site selection and nest-entrance orientation in Sprague's Pipit. Wilson Bulletin 109:462-469.

Tacha, R. W. 1975. A survey of rail populations in Kansas, with emphasis on Cheyenne Bottoms. M.S. thesis, Kansas State College, Fort Hays, KS.

Tanner, R. W. 1953. Ecology of the Virginia and king rails and the sora in Clay County, Iowa. Ph.D. dissertation, Iowa State College, Ames, IA.

Thornton, F. G. 1982. Concealment as a factor in nest site selection by seven species of Anatidae in Utah. M.S. thesis, University of Guelph, ONT.

Walkinshaw, L. H. 1937. The Virginia Rail in Michigan. Auk 54:464-475.

Weller, M. W., and C. S. Spatcher. 1965. Role of habitat in the distribution and abundance of marsh birds. Department of Zoology and Entomology Special Report Number 43, Agricultural and Home Economics Experiment Station, Iowa State University, Ames, IA.

Wiens, J. A. 1970. Avian populations and patterns of habitat occupancy at the Pawnee site, 1968-1969. U.S. International Biological Program, Grassland Biome Technical Report 63. Colorado State University, Fort Collins, CO.

Wiens, J. A. 1973. Pattern and process in grassland bird communities. Ecological Monographs 43:236-270.

Winter, M. 1994. Habitat selection of Baird's Sparrows in the northern mixed-grass prairie. Diplomarbeit der Fakultät für Biologie der Universität Türbingen, Türbingen, Germany.

Winter, M. 1999a. Relationship of fire history to territory size, breeding density and habitat of Baird's Sparrow in North Dakota. Studies in Avian Biology 19:171-177.

Winter, M. 1999b. Nesting biology of Dickcissels and Henslow's Sparrows in Missouri prairie fragments. Wilson Bulletin 111:515-527.

Winter, S. L., J. R. Cully, Jr., and J. S. Pontius. 2003. Breeding season avifauna of prairie dog colonies and non-colonized areas in shortgrass prairie. Transactions of the Kansas Academy of Science 106:129-138.

Yerkes, T. 2000. Nest-site characteristics and brood habitat selection of redheads: an association between wetlands characteristics and success. Wetlands 20:575-580.

Zimmerman, J. L. 1977. Virginia rail (*Rallus limicola*), p. 46-56. In G. C. Sanderson [ed.], Management of migratory shore and upland game birds in North America. International Association of Fish and Wildlife Agencies, Washington, DC.American Ornithologists' Union. 1998. Check-list of North American Birds. 7th ed. American Ornithologists' Union, Washington, DC.

U.S. Department of the Interior
U.S. Fish & Wildlife Service
Route 1, Box 166
Shepherdstown, WV 25443

http://www.fws.gov

June 2006

www.ingramcontent.com/pod-product-compliance
Lightning Source LLC
Chambersburg PA
CBHW081238280526
45787CB00006B/2703

* 9 7 8 1 5 0 7 7 5 2 1 3 5 *